THE CHURCH OF
THE HOLY SEPULCHRE
IN JERUSALEM

THE CHURCH OF
THE HOLY SEPULCHRE
IN JERUSALEM

CHARLES COÜASNON, O.P.

ARCHITECT D.P.L.G.

TRANSLATED FROM THE ORIGINAL FRENCH BY

J.-P. B. AND CLAUDE ROSS

THE SCHWEICH LECTURES
OF THE BRITISH ACADEMY
1972

LONDON
PUBLISHED FOR THE BRITISH ACADEMY
BY THE OXFORD UNIVERSITY PRESS
1974

Oxford University Press, Ely House, London W. 1

GLASGOW NEW YORK TORONTO MELBOURNE WELLINGTON
CAPE TOWN IBADAN NAIROBI DAR ES SALAAM LUSAKA ADDIS ABABA
DELHI BOMBAY CALCUTTA MADRAS KARACHI LAHORE DACCA
KUALA LUMPUR SINGAPORE HONG KONG TOKYO

ISBN 0 19 725938 3

*Printed in Great Britain
at the University Press, Oxford
by Vivian Ridler
Printer to the University*

PREFACE

THE Dominican establishment in Jerusalem, the École Biblique, has a distinguished history of learned research, watchful defence of Jerusalem's antiquities, and generous help to visiting scholars. Situated a short way outside the Damascus Gate, it has had its full share of the troubles that have passed over the city, but its great library has remained intact, and it has nobly maintained scholarly standards throughout all the tribulations of the times. The Dominican fathers, H. Vincent and F.-M. Abel, in their *Recherches de topographie, d'archéologie et d'histoire de Jérusalem* (1912–26) gave an account of the problems of Jerusalem that will always be the basis of further researches. Père Charles Coüasnon stands in this great tradition, and above all he is connected with work on the restoration of the church of the Holy Sepulchre. It is a building that has indeed suffered many changes. A Constantinian foundation, it was twice destroyed and rebuilt before the Crusaders took it in hand and built their choir, in a transitional style between Romanesque and Gothic. Respected by Saladin at his conquest, the church remained much as the Crusaders left it, with some repairs carried out in 1719 under great difficulties, repairs that included a reduction in height of the bell tower. Then on 12 October 1808 a fire broke out in one of the chapels of the Rotunda, and spread through the whole building. Restoration was entrusted to a Greek architect, Comnenos, who rebuilt much of the apse and encased the pillars of the Rotunda and the choir in rubble pillars faced with stone. These and other changes served to hold the building together, though producing the clumsy, ill-lit interior with which many of us were long familiar. Then in 1927 a severe earthquake shook Jerusalem, and cracks appeared in many parts of the building. Mr. William Harvey was called in to survey it, and produced a report that added much to our knowledge of the structure, but little was done to cope with the urgent needs of repair. The twelfth-century dome over the crossing was taken down and reconstructed, and the southern façade encased in steel scaffolding, which remained supporting it for some forty years.

It was after the Second World War that the problem was seriously tackled. A combined undertaking between the various churches owning different parts of the complex of buildings required diplomatic skill of a high order. A plan prepared by Anastas K. Orlandos, Jean Trouvelot, and Édouard Utudjian, aided by Leonidas Collas, Charles Coüasnon, and Diran Voskeritchian, was eventually agreed upon in 1959. Its execution was often threatened by new disagreements, and some of the detail represents unhappy compromises, but the Crusading choir can now be seen with its twin columns restored, its triforium opened up, and the scaffolding at last removed from its southern entrance. Work is now in progress on the interior of the Rotunda.

No one has probably had such a close knowledge of the church, from foundations to roof top, as has Père Coüasnon. Thanks to him, the various buildings on the site can now be planned with new authority, and the existing workmanship assigned to different periods of construction. And if one stands with him among its foundations, where Golgotha can be seen as a hillock rising from the gulley that separates it from the hillside of the tomb, it is clear that this is a site that accords with all the known evidence about the Crucifixion. The centre of Christian aspirations over many centuries, the church of the Holy Sepulchre has now most happily found its historian.

T. S. R. BOASE

CONTENTS

LIST OF PLATES

at end

LIST OF FIGURES

INTRODUCTION

WHEN one talks of the Holy Sepulchre in Jerusalem, one is speaking not only of the Tomb of Christ, but of a whole group of religious buildings of Constantinian origin, enclosing the traditional sites of the Crucifixion and of the Sepulchre of Jesus. All who visit these Holy Places are surprised by the complexity of the monument that covers them.

The Church is, as it were, engulfed by the city; one approaches without seeing it. Coming from the west, one descends steps through a covered passage; from the east, one arrives through a low door into a little courtyard longer than it is wide, measuring about 30×15 metres and, at the end of it, there rises a façade 20 metres high (Pl. I). Passing through the doorway, one finds oneself in the transept of a Romanesque galleried church: that is to say, around the great internal spaces, the galleries of the first storey overlie those at ground level. But this church has no nave: in the place where one would normally expect to see the nave there is a Rotunda, measuring more than twenty metres in diameter. At its centre, a little baroque edifice marks the traditional site of Christ's Tomb (Pl. II).

The transept was built by the Crusaders during the first half of the twelfth century and it was consecrated on 15 July 1149; but the Rotunda is earlier. A study of the Crusaders' work will follow later, in its proper chronology; for the time being let us contemplate the Rotunda.

This circular edifice is ranged around the Tomb, which, to this day, remains the central feature, in relation to which the whole structure is organized. Is not this arrangement of the Rotunda, *vis-à-vis* the Tomb, an argument in favour of the antiquity of the monument? Or is the Rotunda only a composition, superimposed on an earlier layout which has disappeared?

A great many hypotheses have arisen around the question as to what might have been the appearance of the original monument. We can get an idea of these by looking at the recapitulatory diagram published by Professor Testini (Fig. 1).[1] One can reduce all these attempts at reconstitution to two types. Many people maintain that the Tomb was located inside a completely circular building, similar to the mausoleum erected in Rome

---

[1] P. Testini, 'L'Anastasis alla luce delle recenti indagini', *Oriens Antiquus*, iii (1964), p. 263.

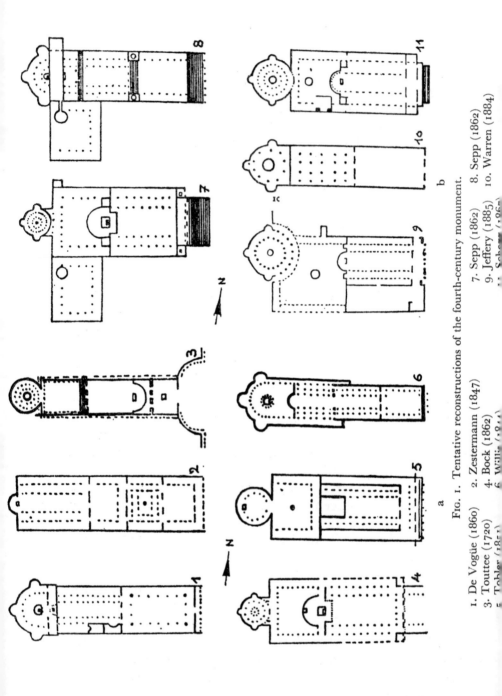

Fig. 1. Tentative reconstructions of the fourth-century monument.

a

1. De Vogüe (1860)   2. Zestermann (1847)
3. Touttee (1720)   4. Bock (1862)
5. Tobler (1851)   6. Willis (1844)

b

7. Sepp (1862)   8. Sepp (1862)
9. Jeffery (1885)   10. Warren (1884)
11. Schramm (1860)

over the Tomb of Constantia, the daughter of Constantine (Fig. 2). This round church, joined to the Basilica of St. Agnes, is named St. Constance. Father Vincent and Mr. Conant are among those who have adopted this conclusion.[1]

Others hold the view that the Tomb was venerated in a courtyard, in the open air. Willis, as long ago as 1844, had already postulated this hypothesis. It was revived more recently by Dalman and by Dyggve, the latter of whom thought, thereby,

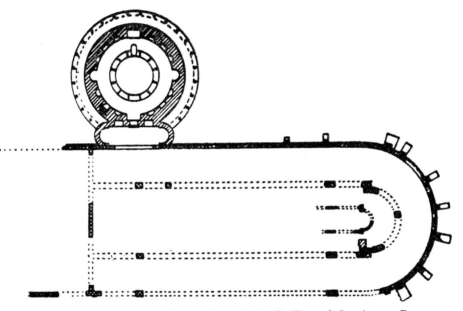

FIG. 2. The Mausoleum of Constantia and the Basilica of St. Agnes, Rome. (*Krautheimer, Cah. Arch.* 11; *after Rivista di archeologia cristiana, XLVII, no. 3-4*)

to reapply his theory of the 'Basilica discoperta', 'la basilique hypètre', that is to say, open to the sky. Professor Krautheimer has reintroduced this theory even more recently (Fig. 3).[2] Certainly, the silence of Bishop Eusebius of Caesarea on the subject of the Rotunda, in the description he gave of the work of Constantine in the year 337, after the death of the Emperor, leads one to believe that, at that date, no Rotunda as yet existed. Yet, on the other hand, we have to concede that the Rotunda was in existence at the end of the fourth century, since Egeria, in her narrative of her travels, speaks of the religious ceremonies which were celebrated there around the year 395.

[1] Emerson H. Swift, *Roman Sources of Christian Art*, figs. 38 and 39, p. 43.
[2] R. Krautheimer, *Early Christian and Byzantine Architecture*, p. 39, fig. 16; after Suzanne S. Alexander: 'Studies in Constantinian Church Architecture', *Rivista di archeologia cristiana*, An. 67 (1971), pp. 281 ff.

Archaeological research and works carried out in the Church of the Holy Sepulchre during the last ten years and more permit the possibility of a solution to this problem, which I shall put before you. I shall also propose a reconstitution of the shape of the primitive mausoleum, basing my ideas on architectural features which can be attributed to the fourth century and which are so numerously preserved in the existing Rotunda.

Before beginning this study, I should like to render homage to those who have made it possible. Firstly, a tribute to the Religious Communities, for whom the work on the Holy Sepulchre

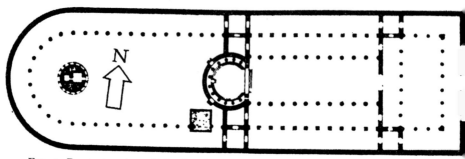

Fig. 3. Reconstruction of the fourth-century Holy Sepulchre by R. Krautheimer.
(*After R. Krautheimer, Early Christian and Byzantine Architecture*)

has been carried out. Likewise, homage to those who have directed and accomplished that work. What I shall have to say about the Holy Sepulchre is based on the results of an important common enterprise, brought to fulfilment by a group of architects and by an archaeologist, Father Virgilio Corbo, a Franciscan. The latter has been able to excavate all that part of the monument situated to the north of the Rotunda and to follow the digging carried out elsewhere in the church. He has published the results of his work in the *Liber Annuus*, the Review of the Franciscan Institute for Biblical Studies,[1] accompanied by an abundant and remarkable documentation. Apart from a few details, I share his view that the whole of the masonry-work on the ground level of the Rotunda is of the fourth century, which introduces a truly new element into the problem of the Holy Sepulchre.

The three architects who directed the work were acting on behalf of the three Religious Communities who share the Holy Sepulchre; Mr. Anastas K. Orlandos was the architect of the Greek Orthodox Patriarchate of Jerusalem; Mr. Stikas and, later, Messrs. Chatzidakis, Moutzopoulos, and Salomonides

[1] Fr. Virgilio Corbo, *Liber Annuus*, xii (1962), xiv (1963–4), xv (1964–5), xix (1969).

have succeeded him in their turns. Monsieur Jean Trouvelot is the architect for the Custodian of the Holy Land, the Representative of the Roman Catholic Community, while Mr. Édouard Utudjian is the architect of the Armenian Patriarchate.

The Technical Office is the joint executive organ of the whole undertaking; Leo Collas, Diran Voskeritchian, and myself were in charge of it, but Athanase Ekonomopoulos has now replaced Leo Collas.

I

HISTORICAL BACKGROUND

1. *The Tomb at the time of the Apostles*

THE history of the Holy Sepulchre starts with the burial of the
body of Jesus. The New Testament texts prove that he really
was buried—a fact that certain critics have sought to deny in
various ways.[1]

Jesus was tried, condemned to death, and handed over to his
accusers by Pilate. 'They took Jesus, and led him away', St.
John tells us, 'and he bearing his cross went forth into a place
called the place of a skull, which is called in the Hebrew Golgotha' (John 19: 16b–17). 'Now, in the place where he was
crucified there was a garden; and in the garden a new sepulchre,
wherein was never man yet laid. There laid they Jesus therefore
because of the Jews' preparation day; for the sepulchre was
nigh at hand' (John 19: 41–2). 'The place where Jesus was
crucified', St. John informs us, 'was nigh to the city . . . ' (John
19: 20b). It was evidently by the side of a fairly populous
thoroughfare, since, St. John tells us, 'many Jews' read the
placard which Pilate had had placed on the cross (John 19:
20a), while, according to St. Matthew and St. Mark, 'they that
passed by reviled Him' (Matthew 27: 39; Mark 15: 29).

From these texts, it is clear that the gibbet was located outside
the town and, probably, near one of the gates; this is also suggested by the following words from the Epistle to the Hebrews:
'wherefore Jesus . . . suffered without the gate' (Hebrews 13: 12).
As to the garden, where the tomb was, it stood in the immediate
vicinity of the gibbet.

To this topographical preciseness, which testifies to a good
knowledge of the places, we can add further testimony of
another kind from St. Mark. While Joseph of Arimathea was in
the act of burying the body of Jesus 'in a sepulchre which was
hewn out of a rock' (Mark 15: 46b), those saintly women, 'Mary
Magdalene and Mary the mother of Joses beheld where he was
laid' (Mark 15: 47). In this narrative, which draws on the
evidence of the holy women, the Evangelist asserts the reality of
the burial of Jesus and, since they were present at the time He

[1] Fr. Pierre Benoit, *Passion et Résurrection du Seigneur*, pp. 258–62.

was placed in the tomb, the first Christian Church Community of Jerusalem must, through them, have known of its location.

This story of the burial of Jesus can reasonably be accepted as being historically true and one must conclude that 'the first Church of Jerusalem had an exact, and well-attested, knowledge of the location of the tomb of Jesus'.[1] Moreover, it is evident that many details of the Gospels are more easily explainable if, at the moment the texts were written, there still existed a living knowledge of the tomb.

To summarize: the new tomb (Matthew, John), was hewn in the rock (Matthew, Mark, Luke), in a garden (John), near to the city (John), the owner of which was known (Matthew), being Joseph of Arimathea (Matthew, Mark, Luke, John), a well-known counsellor (Mark, Luke); in the tomb, the mortuary couch is situated on the right-hand side (Mark), while the low door obliges one to stoop to look inside (John). All these facts, so solid, prove that the authors of the Gospel texts knew the places, had seen the tomb, and had been into it.

How can one admit that St. Luke who '. . . had perfect understanding of all things from the very first . . . ' never visited the tomb? He arrived in Jerusalem around the year 58, accompanying St. Paul. He was aware of the ancient text of the story of the visit of the holy women to the Tomb, since he used it himself in his own writings. Thus, the knowledge of this tradition is inseparable from a knowledge of the site to which it is attached. It appears difficult to admit, therefore, that Luke never saw the tomb.

In short, Jesus really was placed in the tomb and the holy women saw where he was placed. Through them, the Christian Community of Jerusalem knew where the tomb was located and the authors of the Gospels speak of it as a well-known place. Thus, one can say that the tradition was already established when St. Luke came to Jerusalem in A.D. 58 and that he became familiar with this tradition. To be accepted, the tradition must have been very solid since, in A.D. 58, the city had already grown to the north and to the west and, therefore, the quarter containing the tomb was, by then, inside the walls. A tomb inside the city would have seemed very improbable if the tradition had not already existed, and so precisely, to bear witness to the authenticity of the venerated site. How did this ancient tradition come down intact to the fourth century? There we have quite a different problem.

[1] L. Schenke, *Le Tombeau vide et l'annonce de la Résurrection*, p. 103.

2. *The authenticity of the traditional site*

One cannot actually prove that the present site, which has been considered the authentic one since the year 326, is, beyond any doubt, the same as that venerated by the Christian Community in apostolic times. We shall see that its identification at the time it was rediscovered still remains somewhat confused. Nevertheless, if its authenticity cannot be proved, it remains possible, and even probable.

In order to stay within the bounds of a possible authenticity, it will suffice to prove that the actual site was, in fact, outside the city at the time of Christ. If, in addition, one can establish the fact that the ancient tradition had been kept alive and binding in the Christian Community of Jerusalem, then this authenticity also becomes probable.

To prove that the actual site was outside the city at the time of Christ involves problems of archaeology and of history. What do we know of the changes in the positioning of the northern walls of the city between the Maccabaean Era and the taking of Jerusalem by Titus? What were the city limits at the time of Christ? The excavations carried out in Jerusalem by Miss Kenyon around the city, and those nearer to the Sepulchre in the Mauristan quarter, have precisely clarified this problem, and I may be permitted to rely on her findings.

We know the positions of the succession of walls forming the northern limits of the city from an account given by Flavius Josephus in his work *The Jewish War*. He describes the final attack by Titus, in the year 70, against the northern front of the city. In his account, he speaks of three walls that the attacker had to besiege, one after the other, and provides the reference-points which enable us to locate them. Three walls; this does not mean that there was actually a triple encirclement, but only that these three lines of fortifications marked the successive growths of the city (Pl. III).

The 'first Wall', that is to say the most ancient one, is that located the furthest inside the city, and which Titus reached last. It started at the Tower of Hippicus, that is to say from the Citadel, and, passing across the central valley, the Tyropoeon, joined up with the Western Gate of the Temple. This was, more or less, a direct line east–west. It is generally agreed that this line corresponds approximately to the existing Street of David, although, in fact, there is no proof of this. This wall would have been of Maccabaean origin, according to Miss

Kenyon, and not of the time of the Kings.[1] The Holy Sepulchre is situated 230 metres to the north of the line of this 'first Wall'.

The 'third Wall', the most recent and outermost, is that which Titus attacked the first. In the year 70 it constituted the northern front of the city. It was the work of King Herod Agrippa the First and was started in the year 41, only eleven years after the Passion. The sub-foundations of the Damascus Gate, studied in 1964–6 by Basil Hennessy of the British School of Archaeology, belong to the 'third Wall'.[2] The traditional site of the Tomb and of Golgotha were thus, at that time, right inside the city, 350 metres to the south of the Damascus Gate, but, be it noted, this was after the Passion.

It is thus evident that the layout of the 'second Wall' is the one on which everything depends. It was the City Wall at the time of Christ. 'It started', Josephus tells us,[3] 'from the Gate Gennath which belonged to the first wall. Encircling the only northern quarter, it extended as far as the Antonia.' The date of its construction is uncertain. If it is prior to Herod the Great, it could still belong to the Maccabaean period. In reconstructing its alignment, the reference-point of the Antonia is precise, but the 'Gate Gennath' is not mentioned elsewhere. Where can one place it? What is certain is that it belonged to the 'first Wall'. An old wall, discovered under the German Church, and which was believed to be part of the 'second Wall' has, only recently, been attributed by Dr. Lux to the second century. Thus, we must necessarily repudiate an alignment climbing towards the west as far as the Citadel and, therefore, not place the 'Gate Gennath' near to the Hippicus Tower.

The 'second Wall' should, more probably, be looked for under the Souk, as Miss Kenyon has already suggested, following her excavations in the Mauristan quarter. The most likely alignment may well have started from the Gate Gennath, but this Gate opened into the 'first Wall', not near to the Hippicus Tower, but 250 metres further east. Starting from there, and running perpendicularly to the 'first Wall', the 'second Wall' followed a straight south–north line, which the Cardo Maximus of Hadrian, as well as the present Souk, have preserved until today. The 'Gate Gennath' could have been 'that gate in the

---

[1] Kathleen M. Kenyon, *Jerusalem: Excavating 3,000 years of History* (Thames and Hudson, 1967).

[2] J. B. Hennessy, 'Excavations at Damascus Gate Jerusalem, 1964–66', *Levant* ii (1970), p. 22.

[3] André Parrot, *Golgotha et Saint Sépulcre*, p. 10.

ancient rampart' (the 'first Wall') that Father Vincent[1] imagined
to be on the site of the present Bashourah Gate.

After running for 300 metres in the direction south–north,
the wall turned eastward to rejoin the Antonia. The present
site of the Holy Sepulchre is 120 metres to the west of this line.
It is thus outside the wall and could be authentic. Another gate
probably opened into the 'second Wall' nearby, and the road-
way passing close to the gibbet came out there; but of this we
have no proof. Nor is the name of this gate to be found in the
gate-names listed by Nehemiah. Nothing of this quarter, including the 'first Wall', would seem to have belonged to the city of
Nehemiah's time. Thus, the authenticity of the Holy Sepulchre
is shown to be possible, since the actual site is most certainly
outside the city as it existed before the year 41.

Let us now return to the problem of the strong and compelling
tradition, which might have enabled the site of the Tomb to be
fixed without error. It should be said, first of all, that the emplacement identified by Bishop Macarius in the fourth century
is acceptable and possible from an archaeological point of view;
therefore, the tradition on which the Bishop relied could be
accurate.

Despite the very serious upheavals suffered by the city of
Jerusalem—the first Jewish Revolt in the year 66; the attack by
Titus in 70; the second Jewish Revolt in 132—notwithstanding
all these disasters and the time which had elapsed, it would seem
probable that the ancient tradition of the location of the Tomb
had not been lost. The information given to the Empress Helena,
when she came to Jerusalem to preside over the start of the
construction-work, was probably correct. This ancient tradition,
having become established, was transmitted, seemingly intact,
down to Bishop Macarius, guaranteed by the continuity of the
Christian Community of Jerusalem and by the unbroken succession of Bishops, from the death of St. James the Less, first
Bishop of Jerusalem, who was stoned to death in the year 62.

This tradition must have been precise and convincing; if
not, another, more probable, site would have been invented—
especially after the construction of Aelia Capitolina. But, since
this tradition affirmed that the Tomb had been buried under
the Temple of Aphrodite, in the forum in the very centre of the
city, it was unthinkable that another site could be established
elsewhere, however much the better adapted, or more probable,
it might be.

[1] Fr. Vincent, *Jérusalem nouvelle*, p. 55.

As to the location of the Tomb itself, in the very centre of the city, this must have been just as disconcerting for St. Helena as it can be for tourists today to come upon the Church of the Holy Sepulchre deeply concealed in the old city. The 'Garden Tomb' of General Gordon would have been much more satisfying. But the Jerusalem tradition had established a site so difficult to admit, that it must have taken all the weight of an extremely strongly rooted tradition to make such an improbability acceptable. We may thus affirm that it is possible that the location of the Tomb is authentic, and it is even very probable that it is the true one. But we cannot have an absolute certainty of this.

3. *The town plan of Aelia Capitolina*

The construction of Aelia Capitolina engulfed the Tomb. Why? I do not believe that one can read into this fact any anti-Christian gesture of the Roman administration. It was, rather, by chance, or even through an act of Providence, that the Tomb came, thereby, to be conserved. The topography of the ground sufficed to justify the earthworks which were carried out for the building of the forum and its annexes.

Jerusalem had been taken by Hadrian in the year 134 and, from 135 onwards, Rufus Tineius, Legate of Palestine, rebuilt the Roman colony of Aelia Capitolina. On the site of the destroyed temple he erected statues of the Capitoline Zeus and of the Emperor. The layout of the city was modified to accord with Roman style, by adding the Cardo Maximus and the Decumanus. The plan of Jerusalem shown in the Madaba mosaic (Pl. IV) gives us an idea of the layout of Aelia Capitolina. The Damascus Gate, although repaired, was, from then on, no more than a monumental arch at the entrance to an unfortified city.

The Cardo Maximus was then constructed, following the line of the 'second Wall' along its south–north stretch, after which it continued in a straight line to the neighbourhood of the Damascus Gate (Pl. V). It is said that there was a circus there with a column in its centre—hence the name, 'Bab el 'Amoud', still given to the Damascus Gate. From the circus, the street of the Tyropoeon also started. This was not a part of the Roman planning, but existed as a natural thoroughfare before Hadrian. The Cardo Maximus, so laid out, continued beyond the Decumanus and crossed the city, following the hillside almost horizontally. The Decumanus runs perpendicular to the Cardo

Maximus and follows the alignment of the 'first Wall'. The tetrapyle occupied, approximately, the site of the Gate 'of the Gardens'.

The horizontal plane of the Cardo Maximus, before arriving at the tetrapyle, had to cut through a fairly deep valley, precisely following the line along which the 'first Wall' had been built. Miss Kenyon's site 'C' and the drilling done by Miss Lux under the German church are, respectively, on the southern and northern flanks of this valley, which has completely disappeared under the enormous fills of rubble which have been found, and which can be dated as of the end of the first century and the beginning of the second. The Forum of Hadrian was situated on the northern flank of the same valley. It was a convenient spot for the development of a horizontal space perpendicular to the Cardo Maximus. To the west, the Forum terminated up against the general slope of the hill, while, to the north, it was bounded by embanked ground where quarries had existed.

The Tomb and Golgotha were situated at the precise western extremity of the horizontal plane of the Forum, at the spot where the ground rose. In order to build the Temple of Aphrodite there, it was necessary to make a levelling some 4·50 metres above the Forum, partly by cutting away the hill and partly with a filling. The Tomb was buried under these earthworks, but without being disturbed. This was due to the topography of the ground and not to any ill will of the administration which, far from destroying, saved it. The same terracing rose to the north of the Forum like a sort of podium, under which Golgotha likewise became buried. The civic basilica of Aelia Capitolina probably occupied this space; but here I am in the realm of hypothesis only.

4. *The discovery of the Tomb*

In the year 324, when Constantine, after his victory over Licinius, became the sole master of the Roman Empire, the town-plan of Aelia Capitolina had not changed for nearly 200 years, while the Church Community of Jerusalem had then existed for 300 years. In 325, Constantine convoked the Nicaean Council, with the object of re-establishing the unity of the Faith, which had been compromised by the Arian heresy. Bishop Macarius of Jerusalem came to the Council and requested the Emperor to disinter the Tomb of the Lord, which, according to tradition, was buried under the Temple of Aphrodite, to the west of Hadrian's Forum. Constantine replied favourably to Macarius's wish, and commanded the razing of the pagan temple in order to rediscover the Tomb.

The source-material which we possess concerning the early history of the Holy Sepulchre as a monument, is contained in one of the works of Eusebius of Caesarea, his *Life of Constantine*. It is a work of edification and of panegyric; but, despite the declamatory and emphatic style of the writing, the documentation of Eusebius is generally considered to be precise. He himself declaimed a panegyric on the Emperor in this same Basilica of Jerusalem, which he described, shortly afterwards, in his *Life of Constantine*. He is, therefore, a serious witness and I shall quote him extensively.[1]

Here is how he gives us the Emperor's decision to rediscover the Tomb: 'He deemed it necessary to bring to light, in Jerusalem, the blessed place of the Resurrection of the Saviour, so that all might be able to see and venerate it.' He goes on, talking of the works of Hadrian: 'No efforts had been spared to pile up earth brought there from elsewhere; they concealed the landscape by raising the level of the ground and by covering it with flagstones: the Divine Grotto thus became buried under a mass of packed earth.'[2] On the ground which had been thus prepared, the Temple of Aphrodite was built.

The text which I have just quoted does not have the emphatic and polemical style which informs the work as a whole. He describes an earthwork in a somewhat technical manner. Neither 'the impious ones', nor 'the atheists', nor 'the whole race of Demons' enter into this passage. One constructs an embankment, to support a paved surface, on a higher level. I would be inclined to treat this as a technical Report on Hadrian's works, prepared on behalf of the Christian Community and preserved by it.

Once taken, the Emperor's decision was immediately put into execution. The temple was destroyed and the earthworks removed: 'And behold!' says Eusebius, 'the place which had witnessed the Resurrection of the Saviour reappeared, surpassing all hopes.'

How was the Tomb identified? Here, the text of Eusebius remains obscure. Monsieur Jean Lassus[2] translates: 'the grotto, Holy of Holies, *presents an aspect like unto* the Resurrection of the

---

[1] Bardy, *Sources chrétiennes*, no. 73; Eusebius of Caesarea, ecclesiastical writer, born at Caesarea in Palestine about 275–280, bishop of Caesarea in 340.

[2] Jean Lassus, *Revue de l'histoire des religions*, vol. 172, p. 135, French translation of the texts of Eusebius of Caesarea.

Saviour'. Father Abel[1] translated otherwise: 'the grotto, Holy of Holies, *reflected in a striking manner* the return to life of the Saviour.' Indeed, it was as if the Tomb, like its former Holy Occupant, had arisen from the dead, returning to the light of day after 300 years of burial. The text of Eusebius is somewhat confused by the allegory, but it clearly assumes that 'the divine grotto', 'the sacred cavern', the holy Tomb was, from then on, considered authentic. We have earlier concluded that this authenticity is not impossible, and even that the chances are that it might be exact. Nevertheless, in spite of everything, there remains some room for uncertainty.

5. *The two construction sites*

Once the Tomb had been disinterred during 326/7, work on the Rotunda ought to have been started immediately. Are there not grounds, however, for believing that work on the Basilica, which was completed in 335, had been started before the other?

In the writings of Eusebius one can, seemingly, identify two construction sites. Indeed, when Constantine took his decision to restore the most holy place of the Resurrection to the view, and for the veneration, of all, he commanded, at the same time, that one should 'raise a house of prayer', that is to say, a church, the Basilica itself, which would become the major church of Jerusalem. While the clearing of the Tomb was under way, work was immediately started on the Basilica, which would be finished well before the Rotunda, and would take the name 'Basilica of Constantine', to which would be added later that of 'Mar Constantin', that is to say, 'St. Constantine'.

Likewise, in the administrative arrangements made in preparation for the constructions, there are two distinct directives, one concerning the sanctuary to be raised around the Tomb and, on the other hand, that which dealt with more general arrangements relative to the work on the Basilica. According to Eusebius, the Imperial decision on the subject of the Tomb was as follows:

The Prince, uniting abundant munificence with the dictates of piety which inspire him, commands that there shall be erected around the Grotto of Salvation a sanctuary of a magnificence worthy of his wealth and of his crown.

---

[1] Fr. Abel, *Jérusalem nouvelle*, chaps. VI and VII, p. 206, translation of the texts of Eusebius of Caesarea. Unless otherwise indicated, all the texts quoted here are taken from this French translation.

Thus, the Rotunda around the Tomb was, indeed, part of the original project of Constantine, but its realization would take a long time, because of the magnitude of the work to be carried out. It would be necessary to disengage 'the Holy Grotto' from the hill where it had been buried, while retaining the mass of rock surrounding it, and to level around it a circular space of thirty-five metres in diameter. This was an enormous undertaking; the stone extracted, amounting to a volume of nearly five thousand cubic metres, was hewn, by pickaxe, in the form of dressed blocks which were used for the construction of the monument. Excavations have revealed remains of this extraction of stone. For these reasons, Eusebius of Caesarea, who died in the year 340, never saw the completed Rotunda.

The description he has left us of the monument, as he saw it, which we can read in his *Life of Constantine*, written after 337, the date of the death of the Emperor, can be summarized as follows: 'Above all, he embellished the sacred Grotto, the divine monument as the principal point of the whole. . . . The Emperor's magnificence in decorating this centrepiece with selected columns of abundant ornamentation, made the venerable grotto shine under a glittering adornment.'[1] There is here no question of the Rotunda.

Thus, the work carried out on the Tomb itself in the year 337 consisted only of decorative work. The mass of rock, disengaged from the hill, was furnished with columns and shone under its precious decorations. The Tomb, so arranged, was that which we have seen on the ampullae of Monza (Pl. VI). It would later be sheltered within the Rotunda, but, meanwhile, it was worshipped by pilgrims in a courtyard while, all around, the construction of the Rotunda was continuing.

Eusebius's description goes on to state that there stretched from the Tomb towards the east, 'a vast space, open to the sky, paved with beautiful stone and surrounded on three sides by long porticos (Pl. VII). On the side directly facing the grotto, that is to say the eastern side, lay the Basilica, rising to a considerable height and very extensive both in length and in breadth.'[1] Eusebius then goes on to describe in detail the splendour of this building, the consecration of which had taken place on 17 September of the year 335, and not on the 14th, the liturgical date which still today commemorates this event.

The work on the Basilica, which Eusebius had seen completed while work on the Rotunda was continuing, had been the

[1] See note 1, p. 14.

subject of a separate directive from that of the sanctuary destined to shelter the Tomb. As regards the Basilica, the Bishop of Jerusalem was to take 'all necessary measures to construct a church which, not only in its ensemble might surpass in loveliness all others, but also the details of which should be of such a quality that their excellence would transcend in beauty anything that the other cities of the Empire could show.' Administrative arrangements would be made to bring to Jerusalem artists, workmen, and precious materials. The Emperor went as far as concerning himself with the details of the ceilings: 'I require of you, if you please, that the ceilings of the Basilica shall be decorated with coffers, or any other ornamentation. If coffering is preferred, it could be enhanced with gold. . . .'

It does, therefore, seem probable that there were, indeed, two construction sites; that of the Basilica, which progressed rapidly, and that of the Rotunda, which was more difficult and, therefore, slower, which is why the Rotunda was not completed at the time of the death of Constantine. We have a further testimony, a much shorter text, dating from the year 333; it may be read in the 'Pilgrim of Bordeaux', who crossed the city from the Zion Gate to the Nablus Gate (i.e. the Damascus Gate).

'To the left', he says, '[there is] the hillock of Golgotha, where the Lord was crucified. A stone's throw from there is the grotto, where His body was placed and arose on the third day.' He says nothing about the Rotunda. He continues: 'ibidem', i.e. on the same spot (that is to say, Golgotha), 'there was recently constructed, on the orders of the Emperor Constantine, a Basilica, a church of admirable loveliness, with reservoirs alongside it from which one draws water and, behind, a baptistry where children are purified.'

The principal church was already nearly completed by the year 333. Just as Eusebius enthusiastically described it, without mentioning a word about the Rotunda, so, likewise, the Pilgrim of Bordeaux admired the new church built by Constantine and saw, a stone's throw away from Golgotha, the grotto, the Holy Tomb, standing alone in a courtyard. Our two witnesses, Eusebius and the Pilgrim, corroborate one another.

One must wait until the end of the fourth century to find, in the 'Travel Diary' of Egeria, a description of the liturgical ceremonies celebrated in the Anastasis, that is to say, the Rotunda. The doors are opened, they are closed; the Patriarch enters, the people emerge; we are clearly in a building. The Rotunda around the Tomb is completed; that Rotunda which today still retains its complete layout and even some of its walls, preserved up to a height of eleven metres.

6. *Highlights in the history of the Holy Sepulchre*

During two centuries, the Holy Sepulchre of Jerusalem (Pl. VIII) was to be the most celebrated of pilgrimages, at a time when these were innumerable. Contemporaneously, Palestinian monasticism enjoyed the greatest renown. The Holy Sepulchre's place in iconography is an important one; portrayals of the Holy Tomb adorn a great number of precious objects of Byzantine art. There are, for example, those silver ampullae of Monza and of Bobbio, on which are struck representations of the Tomb, the best that exist.[1] In these religious objects, pilgrims preserved drops of oil from the lamps which burned, day and night, at the Tomb. For the Christian world, Jerusalem was a centre of attraction above all others; as the Cross and the Resurrection are at the centre of the faith, so the hearts of all Christians were in Jerusalem.

But, with the seventh century, misfortunes arrived. The Byzantine and Persian Empires destroyed each other, and Syria, Palestine, Mesopotamia, and Egypt became territory of Islam.

On 4 May 614, the first serious incident occurred. The Persian army of Chosroës Parviz took Jerusalem; the Holy Sepulchre and the other sanctuaries were burned, and a relic of the Cross was carried off by the conquerors. From 622 onwards, Heraclius, sometimes the vanquished, sometimes the victor, re-established his power over Syria and Palestine and then marched on Ctesiphon, where Chosroës was assassinated in February 628. The royal conqueror retook the Cross and brought it back in triumph to Jerusalem on 21 March 628.

The repairs, following on the conflagration of 614, would, by that time, have been partly completed. Modestus, Abbot of Saint Theodosius, in the Judaean desert and later Patriarch, had undertaken this work, which was certainly most difficult, since the Imperial finances scarcely sufficed to defend the territory. The roofing, the decorations, and the furnishings had been destroyed but, on the whole, the great work remained as it was. From the testimony of Arculf, the Frankish Bishop, who came to Jerusalem in 685 and who saw the Holy Sepulchre of Modestus, we know that the buildings which he describes are those of the

---

[1] André Grabar, *Ampoules de Terre Sainte (Monza–Bobbio)*. Photos: Denise Fourmont.

Holy Sepulchre of the fourth century, for many of the details which he gives us concerning the repaired Rotunda are part of those features which we are now able to attribute to the fourth century.

Shortly after 628, the break-up of the Byzantine Empire recommenced. As early as 633, Heraclius, overwhelmed by the Arab invasion, relinquished Syria and carried off to Constantinople the remains of the Cross, which he had brought from Ctesiphon. The Arab invasion reached Palestine in 634 and the Mediterranean coast from Gaza to Caesarea was sacked by the invaders, who came in from the 'Araba. In 635, Damascus was taken and, on 20 August 636, at the Battle of the Yarmuk River, the Byzantine army was annihilated.

In February 638, Jerusalem, although completely isolated, still held out, protected only by its walls. The Saracen horsemen were encamped on the Mount of Olives, where the Caliph Omar came to join them in order to receive the submission of the City, which the Patriarch Sophronius had to surrender to him. It was the end of an epoch: the cultured Byzantine, in his rich robes, placed into the hands of the Bedouin, clothed in patched tunic and camel-skin coat, 'the City of the Sanctuary', 'Beit el-Maqdis'.[1]

Omar dictated a Treaty of Guarantee, the terms of which were: '. . . You are assured of complete safety for your lives, your goods and your churches. The latter will not be occupied by Muslims, nor destroyed, provided you do not rise in revolt together.' Everyone knows the story of Omar at prayer:

The Patriarch and the Caliph came into the city. They went to the Holy Sepulchre and seated themselves in the courtyard between the Rotunda and the Basilica. The hour of prayer arrived and the Caliph sought where he might pray. Sophronius had a prayer-mat laid in the middle of the Basilica and invited his visitor to say his prayers there. 'No', said the Caliph, 'I will not pray here', and, leaving by the eastern door, he finally said his prayers alone on the steps in front of the entrance to the church. 'Knowest thou why', he said to the Patriarch, 'I did not pray inside the church?' 'No', replied Sophronius. 'Well, if I had prayed in the church it would have been lost to thee, for the Believers would have taken it out of thy hands, saying, 'Omar hath prayed here.'[2]

We may, perhaps, ask ourselves if it was not regrettable that Omar left the Basilica to pray, for, had it become a mosque, it

[1] Fr. Abel, *La Prise de Jérusalem, Conférences de Saint-Etienne*, 1910–1911, pp. 124 ff.

[2] Frs. Vincent and Abel, *Jérusalem nouvelle*, French translation of the texts of Eutychius and Yahia, pp. 242 ff.

would have been preserved for us. Remaining Christian, it was systematically demolished by the Sultan Hakim in the year 1009. Muslim anti-Christian fanaticism gradually replaced the beautiful generosity of Omar.

From the seventh to the beginning of the eleventh century, the fourth-century monument, as repaired by Modestus, continued to attract pilgrims in increasing numbers, in spite of the difficulties of that Age of Arms.[1] During those four centuries, the monument was to suffer further misfortunes, before disappearing altogether in 1009.

At the beginning of the ninth century, before 810, an earthquake loosened the timbers installed by Modestus. They had to be replaced, beam by beam, from trunks of cedar wood brought from Cyprus. In 966, following the victories of the Byzantine Empire, rioters set fire to the doors and to the woodwork of the monument. It took ten years to replace the roofing of the Rotunda, while, for twenty years, the Basilica of St. Constantine remained without a roof. One may even wonder whether the roof had been replaced by the time that Hakim gave to a certain Baruch of Ramleh the order to destroy the church of the 'Quiameh', that is to say the Holy Sepulchre, 'until all traces of it have disappeared and to endeavour to uproot its foundations'.[2]

In the Rotunda everything was brought down, 'save only that which was too difficult to demolish'. The 'Qranion', the 'Mar Constantin', and all the dependent buildings of the church were demolished. Above all, 'Ibn Abi Dâher was determined to efface all traces of the Holy Tomb'. The rock-mass, the Holy Grotto, which had been detached and decorated by Constantine, was 'broken up by pickaxe and hammer'. The chronicler continues, 'And indeed, Ibn Abi Dâher hewed out the most of it and carried it off.' The text suggests that, perhaps, a small part of the Tomb escaped destruction. All these details are given us by an Arab chronicler, Yahia, who specifies that 'the destruction started on the Tuesday, five days before the end of the month of Safar, in the year 400 of the Hegira'; that is to say, 18 October 1009.

On that date, the fourth-century monument was wiped out. It would seem, however, that the Rotunda proved very difficult to destroy, since the fourth-century features which escaped demolition are numerous and important. The Arab chronicler

[1] Id. chap. ix § 1, p. 248.
[2] Marius Canard, 'Destruction de l'Église de la Résurrection', *Byzantion*, 1965, pp. 16–43.

saw clearly what had happened, because he emphasized the fact that 'those things which proved too difficult to demolish' were spared. One can imagine the different phases of this operation: having dismantled the timbers and the floor-boards—for wood is always for the taking when it is rare—the superstructures were torn down and the columns overturned, while the outside wall remained more or less intact, being preserved to a height of eleven metres. The restoration work of Constantine Mono-machus only restored its height, and it has so come down to us today.

This restoration followed the peace-treaty of 1030, made between Romanus III Argyropoulos and Dâher, the son of Hakim. It stipulated that the Basileus should rebuild the Church of the Resurrection at his own expense; but delays occured, and the money did not arrive. In 1034, an earthquake wrecked the remaining churches of the Holy City which had not been pre-viously destroyed. It was not until 1042, with the arrival of Constantine Monomachus, that the Imperial Treasury provided the necessary subsidies to permit the work to be finished. The Rotunda was rebuilt in 1048 (Pl. IX).

In Jerusalem, the rule of the Fatimids of Egypt had, since 1072, been replaced by that of the Turkish Seljuks, until the Crusaders occupied the Holy City on 15 July 1099. At that date, the Rotunda of Constantine Monomachus had stood for only fifty-one years. It was a very beautiful monument: to its original layout, there had been added a gallery for women, and an apse, which protruded on the eastern façade. The porticos of the courtyard had been re-erected on the old foundations, while Calvary still occupied the south-eastern angle of the porticos; the great Basilica, however, was not rebuilt.

The Crusader church was simply built on to the Rotunda of Constantine Monomachus (Pl. X). It was constructed in the courtyard and enveloped Calvary. No alteration was made in the Rotunda except for the recess of the apse, which was re-moved, the large archway giving access between the two fea-tures, the Rotunda and the Romanesque church. The galleries of the Crusader church were put on the same level as the galleries of the Rotunda, thus forming one large continuous floor, and creating a considerable amount of space. This monument, which was completed on 15 July 1149, has survived to this day; it was very badly damaged by fire in 1808 and today we are trying to restore to it the appearance it had before the fire.

II

THE ROTUNDA

1. *The courtyard around the Tomb pre-dating the Rotunda*

HAVING taken a quick look at the sixteen centuries of the history of the Holy Sepulchre, noting a number of important dates, let us return to the early years of the monument.

The testimony of the Pilgrim of Bordeaux in 333, together with that of Eusebius of Caesarea between the years 337 and 340, forces us to believe that the Tomb was not, at that time, covered by the Rotunda, but that pilgrims venerated it in a courtyard, dominated on the East by the very high chevet of the Basilica of Constantine. Archaeological evidence, uncovered in 1964, possibly gives us proof of an architectural arrangement around the Tomb, which must be dated to the fourth century, but which is prior to the construction of the Rotunda. This should be the remains of the primitive courtyard.

In 1964, an excavation took place to the south of the Rotunda, in the Chapel of the Three Marys, as well as beneath the staircase and the Diwan of the Armenians. This brought to light a foundation-wall, 95 cm. thick, which we will call Wall F (Pl. XI). Two facings of ashlar rest on a rubble of stone and grey mortar; a completely independent Roman wall passes beneath. A stony fill surrounds the wall, containing Byzantine potsherds of the fourth century.[1] One can reconstruct the operation thus: Wall F was built on the levelled Roman demolition site, and was then wholly surrounded with a fill of rubble from the work-site to a height of less than one metre; these works were carried out in the fourth century (Fig. 4).

If we follow Wall F from its starting-point against the Rotunda, we find it caught up in the foundations of column no. 11, which are later in date and have enveloped it. Thereafter, the wall continues to the south for a length of ten metres, until it turns at a right-angle towards the east. After 2·5 metres, it penetrates the foundations of the thick wall of the principal

---

[1] The name 'Roman masonry' is given to all that stonework which belongs to the buildings constructed by Herod or by Hadrian. The expression 'Byzantine masonry or earthworks', refers to construction of the fourth century; the term, 'palaeo-Christian masonry' would perhaps, have been more apt.

façade which, likewise, have enveloped it. Thus, Wall F is clearly earlier than the work of the Rotunda. Moreover, the foundations of the façade-wall have been constructed afterwards, in the first layer of the Byzantine fill, where there is a foundation trench.

The eastward turn of Wall F continues beyond the façade-wall up to point U, following the same alignment and where the masonry is of the same kind. Then, at point U, we meet with

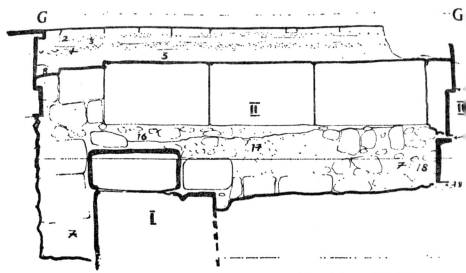

FIG. 4. Chapel of the Three Marys. Section of foundations of Wall F.

the foundation-wall of the southern portico of the courtyard. Consequently, one must assume that, before the building of the façade, the portico had one or two additional spans towards the west, and a return of three or four spans to the north, of which Wall F was the foundation. The façade-wall of the Rotunda was constructed later, 2·5 metres in front of the return spans of the original courtyard.

To the north of the Rotunda, the excavations made by the Reverend Father Corbo in 1968 have brought to light the foundations G, which occupy a position symmetrical to that of Wall F in relation to the Rotunda.[1] The prolongation of the foundations G has been rediscovered under the base of column no. 2, which was removed only in February 1972 (Pl. XII*a*). A foundation flagstone has here been let into the masonry of the foundations G. It is smaller than the other foundation-

[1] Fr. Virgilio Corbo, 'Scavo archeologico a S. Maria-Maddalena', *L.A.* xix (1969), pp. 66 ff.

stones belonging to columns nos. 1 and 3. It measures between 0·95 and 1 metre, instead of 1·30 metres, which could correspond to the foundation of a column in the angle of the ancient portico. But there is no trace of the beginning of any wall running westward; on the contrary, beyond the foundation-stone, to the south, remains of masonry seem to indicate that Wall G continued towards the south, perhaps to join up with Wall F, thus forming a light enclosure in front of the Tomb.

Therefore, the shape of the courtyard in the immediate surroundings of the Tomb cannot be defined; but Wall F, together with the foundations G, form part of the arrangement of the porticos of the courtyard, which were obliterated by the later construction of the Rotunda. The eastward turn of the foundations G is identical to the turn of Wall F; but while the turn in Wall F is at a right-angle, in G the angle is obtuse and the turn aligns itself with the foundation V of the north portico of the courtyard, whose direction is definitely slanted, which, incidentally, presents us with a curious anomaly. In the same way that, in F, the foundations of the façade-wall have enveloped the foundation-wall of the south portico, so likewise in G, the façade-wall has been constructed on the foundation of the north portico.

The Reverend Father Corbo carefully noted this detail, and he came to the conclusion that the foundations G were of the Roman era. However, owing to the similarity and symmetry of the foundations F and G, one has to conclude that both are of the fourth century. What *is* of the Roman era can only be the foundations G 1, which are similar to the Roman wall which passes under Wall F. But while, in the Chapel of the Three Marys, these features are superimposed to a height of more than one metre, and, thus, are easily distinguishable, in the Chapel of St. Mary Magdalene there are only some 32–47 cm. between the flagstones and the rock and the features of the different epochs are, therefore, less easy to distinguish.

2. *The courtyards to the north and west of the Rotunda*

Venerated under the open sky during a number of years, the Tomb was, by the end of the fourth century, certainly situated inside a building. According to the evidence of Egeria, the liturgical prayers of Lauds and Vespers were celebrated around the Tomb every day, the doors of the buildings being opened in the morning at cock-crow.[1] The faithful awaited the opening under the porticos of the courtyard, while, in front of the Tomb, choristers and officiants gathered in the chancel.

I have already taken it upon myself to affirm that the plan of the present Rotunda is, at ground level, unchanged, being the same as the original monument. I must now bring you proof of this assertion, by presenting to you certain aspects of the masonry-work of the Rotunda and of its annexes.

The disengagement of masonry, and the excavations carried out by Father Corbo, began in October 1960, in the Franciscan Convent, which occupies all the annexe buildings to the north of the Rotunda. My description will follow, more or less, the chronological order of these discoveries, since I shall begin with these dependencies.[2]

Around the Rotunda, courtyards existed for the lighting and ventilation of the monument. The northern and western court-yards can easily be reconstituted, since all the walls of the fourth century are now visible. Secondary buildings, having a ground-floor and one storey, were constructed along the length of the retaining-walls, which formed a kind of peribolos at the western and northern limits of the general excavation that had been undertaken to detach the Tomb. The northern wall is pre-served to a height of 13 metres and the upper courses are still visible. The building (NOR) (Pl. XI) backing on to it contained monastic cells opening on to the courtyard (ECH) with walls separating one from the other, through which doorways were later pierced. Each cell had a door, opening on to the courtyard, and a little window (Pl. XIIIa). These doors have straight lintels, one course high, relieved by a very flattened arch, a method of construction usually used in Roman Syria. The building had one storey, and the ancient stonework is still visible, to a height of 7 metres, in what remains of the original courtyard.

A stairway in the north-west angle (N) must have been of wood; the existing vaulting is a later addition, probably of the sixth century. Moreover, all the flooring must have been of wood. The seatings for the two ends of a square beam with a side of 40 cm. still remain in the western and eastern walls of the room in the north-east corner (Q); it was a master-beam which sup-ported joists. This room was vaulted later; the vaulting, which

---

[1] The Revd. John Wilkinson, *Egeria's Travels* (S.P.C.K., London, 1971).

[2] Fr. Virgilio Corbo, 'Gli edifici della Santa Anastasis a Gerusalemme', *L.A.* xii (1961–2), pp. 221 ff.

was very flattened, rested on arches built on to the walls of the fourth century, which were thereby strengthened.

The room in the north-east angle was lit by a slanted window (Q), which took its daylight from the corner of the courtyard; another bay window was set in the other wall, but it was partly blocked by the pier of an archway. A last room joined the angle of the wall of the Rotunda, with which it communicated by a doorway (J). These two rooms were, and still are, on a level with the Rotunda. From there, one could emerge into the courtyard up a flight of four steps and through a doorway (S). This doorway was destroyed in the eleventh century by the construction of the small apse of the Chapel of St. Mary. The arrangement of these two rooms reminds one of an annexe for liturgical purposes, such as a sacristy.

The flattened vaulting resting on the opposing walls in the corner room (Q) has already been mentioned. The same arrangement was repeated in the building on the western turn of the courtyard, where the rooms at courtyard level, as well as those on the upper floor, were all modified, their wooden floorboards being removed and replaced by vaulting. It should be noted that these rooms have been seriously damaged by fire. The work of replacing the wooden flooring by vaults would have been earlier than the fire started by the Persians in 614, and could tally with work carried out at the time of Justinian.

The northern courtyard (ECH) narrows as it proceeds southwards between the building on the western turn of the courtyard and the Rotunda, until it reaches the little slanting passage with cradle-shaped vaulting (P), which joins it with the western courtyard (Pl. XIIIb). Here, there is a most interesting example of stone-dressing. The little slanted archway and the large window of the Rotunda share a common keystone, which proves that the masonry-work of the Rotunda and that of the annexe buildings were done at the same time. The retaining wall of the western courtyard is made up of large dressed stones, whose facing has, however, been destroyed by fire.

A flight of eight steps descended from the western toward the northern courtyard (P), there being a difference in level of some 2 metres between the two. Near the centre of the courtyard (between C and H) one again descended four steps, and there were, likewise, four further steps from the courtyard into the Rotunda. This makes a total of 16 steps, with nearly 4 metres difference in level. Thus, the small western apse was buried up to the starting-point of the vaulting, which explains its outward appearance, differing from that of the other two which are more disengaged and need to be buttressed. These small apses are part of the exterior envelope of the Rotunda, which we will now study.

3. *The periphery walls of the Rotunda*[1]

The central space of the Rotunda is engirdled by a large semicircular deambulatory, the outside wall of which is certainly the most spectacular of the fourth-century features preserved within the monument. This wall can be seen, up to a height of more than eleven metres, running almost intact right round the whole edifice. Its internal face is circular, while its exterior is polygonal.

Three small apses, similar to the northern one (C), open into the wall, as well as six windows, whose combined arcs make a full semicircle, thus forming a very large exedra. The distribution of these features along the length of the wall has its own rhythm, independent of the arrangement of the central space, excepting the small apse on the western axis. This freedom of form expresses itself by the wooden ceilings, with their beams and joists. One can only regret that this remarkable specimen of palaeo-Christian architecture is masked by those miserable monastic lodgings.

The great deambulatory forms two arcs on either side of the central space, leading to two archways, which open into entrance-halls, shaped like a transept (F and G), immediately behind the rectilineal wall of the façade (Pl. XIV). The circular central space, built around the Tomb, is tangential to this façade-wall.

The arrangement of the two vestibules is very curious; everything points to the fact that, here, we have the original layout. Therefore, we can attribute to the fourth century the southern and northern walls, with the lintelled doors (J and H); the alignment of the western wall with the pillars of the Rotunda (L and M); the great archway of the southern vestibule (F) and, in the northern vestibule (G), the jambs (X and Y) of the doors set in the façade. The small southern and northern apses (B and C) hug the vestibules (F and G), forming two wings on either side of the central space; they were covered with double-pitched roofs, while the deambulatory roof (P and E) had but one pitch (Pl. XV).

The distribution of the facets of the outside polygonal façade takes no account of the placing of the windows, whose rhythm

[1] All bracketted capital letters in this section refer to the lettering in Plate XI.

depends entirely on the interior setting. It should be observed that a radius, set-off at 45°, passes through a rib of the exterior polygon in a way such as to make an encircling polygon, if completed, of 24 sides, while that around the internal central space would have 12 sides.

These several features, taken as examples, and, on the outside, the vaulted passage (P); the fitting and dressing of the facing-stones (E); the window of the deambulatory of the small northern apse (C)—all these elements that one can see located around the Rotunda, prove that the form of the original monument is still before our eyes.

4. *The interior arrangement of the Rotunda: the twelve columns of Arculf*

If the exterior envelope of the Rotunda has wholly retained the original form of the monument, the interior layout, on the contrary, has been destroyed and then reconstructed. Therefore, it may well have been modified.

Based on the fact that the Tomb does not occupy the geometric centre of the circle of the Rotunda, but is situated in the axis of the small southern and northern apses, it has been assumed that the Rotunda was displaced within the space delimited by the exterior envelope. This hypothesis would maintain that the existing Rotunda, instead of being exactly on the spot of the original Rotunda, had been moved towards the east, until it became tangential to the façade-wall. Furthermore, the original diameter must have been smaller, the Tomb occupying the geometric centre of the circle, when the two small southern and northern apses would then have been in axis with it. Around a circumference of less length one could then have the more easily distributed the twelve columns of Arculf; the whole object of this hypothesis was, indeed, to fit them in.

However, the exterior envelope of the monument which, as we have seen, is intact, does not permit of this hypothesis. The centre of the circle of implantation of the existing Rotunda is, geometrically speaking, the same as that of the great circular wall which surrounds it. Therefore, since this great circular wall belongs, quite certainly, to the original monument and has undergone no modification, the present location of the Rotunda has, likewise, remained unchanged, because the two circles, that of the Rotunda and that of the great wall, cannot be other than concentric.

What, then, are we to do with the twelve columns of Arculf? As I have told you, this Bishop came to Jerusalem in the year 685 and gave a description of the Rotunda which had just been repaired by Modestus. It had, he tells us, twelve very beautiful columns.

The existing layout of the western half of the Rotunda dates from the eleventh century; it comprises two square pillars (L) to the south, joined by an arch, followed by three columns; then come the two square pillars to the west (K), once more three columns, and, finally, the two northern pillars together with their arch (M). The eastern half contains only two groups of two columns and some curious double columns on each side of the large archway. Thus, following the rebuilding by the Mono-machus, there were ten columns, two double columns, and six square pillars.

The recent restoration of all these features, damaged in the fire of 1808, has allowed us to inspect their foundations, which are certainly the original ones. Under the double columns, there were two foundation-stones, nos. 12 (Pl. XVI*a*) and 1, which are identical to those which have been found under columns nos. 3 (Pl. XII*b*), 4, and 5. A projecting square surface has been cut on a large stone slab, but the dimensions of this surface are less than those of the plinth which it should carry. Therefore, the bearing surface has been brought back towards the centre, in order to avoid breaking the edges.

Therefore, the fourth-century columns were in the same places as those of the eleventh century, and, on the two foundation-stones, nos. 12 and 1, the first and twelfth of the columns of Arculf were erected. Thus, there were four groups of three columns, identical to the two existing groups of the western half of the Rotunda.

While the emplacements are the same, the plinths have probably been changed. The majority of the plinths, marked with crosses, are probably not of the fourth century, but plinth no. 3, which bore no cross, could well be the only genuine original one. Plinth no. 2 is very different, and could date from the eleventh century; in any case, it was certainly placed in position at that time, since the mortar used to place it, which has been found underneath it, was characteristic of the mortars of the eleventh century, containing scraps of ceramic larger than those of other eras. Plinth no. 3, on the contrary, rested on a black dusty bed, and only into the edges had mortar of the eleventh century been wedged.

It appeared that, at the time of the work done in the eleventh century, all the plinths had been pushed outwards a little towards the exterior of the Rotunda. The mortar wedging under plinth no. 3 brought us the proof of this, as did also the non-vertical positioning of columns 2 and 3, which we measured with some precision. They were not absolutely upright, but were slightly inclined inwards, while the surface plane of the arches which they carry corresponds well with the dressing of the northern pillar (M). This would indicate that the perpendicularity of the original major construction work coincided with that of the arches. Thus, the plinths having been displaced several centimetres towards the outside of the circle, the columns were consequently slightly inclined, to compensate for this displacement.

The well-preserved state of the original masonry of the northern pillars (M) (Pl. XVI*b*), on which the eleventh-century arches have been set, is very useful in helping to resolve the problem of the layout of the Rotunda, since it gives us the proof that the three pairs of square pillars (L, K, M) truly belong to the original arrangement. Six courses of the northern pair can be dated as of the fourth century; at the sixth course, one can see, on the eastern face, the remains of the springer of an arch which joined the façade-wall behind the columns. This arch across the vestibule is indispensable from the point of view of the construction. Moreover, the eastern face of the northern pillar (M), like that of the southern pillar (L), aligns itself with the archways at the start of the ambulatories and the walls of the vestibules (F and G). This line connects with the exterior envelope and thus completely ties in with the outline of the original plan.

The fourth-century layout, retained after the repairs made by Modestus, thus comprised four groups of four spans, interrupted at the south, west, and north axes (L, K, M). The eleventh century repeated the same arrangement, modified only in the eastern half, where two double columns were set up on either side of the great archway.

The original disposition, at the tangential point between the interior circle and the rectilineal wall of the façade, on the eastern axis, was probably similar to the other three, which would have given the internal layout complete symmetry. There would thus have been, diagonally, four groups of four spans, interrupted at the cardinal points.

Arculf counted the beautiful columns, of which there were

twelve, but the interruptions had the appearance of walls pierced by passages. He evidently did not think it was necessary to mention this; otherwise his complete description would have been: four cardinal base-points and twelve columns (Pl. XVII).

The doorways or passages, leading through the base-points (L, K, M), did not have the same height as the existing arcades. They were apertures with straight lintels, relatively low, leaving above them a large blank space—a veritable wall, which the good Bishop Arculf had no particular reason to admire.

5. *The height of the columns and the interior dimensions*

The uppermost course of the ancient masonry of the great circular wall is visible all round the Rotunda, in the gallery on the upper floor. It is surmounted by several rows of brickwork, forming a continuous band, which takes up the whole thickness of the wall. It marks the starting-point of the additional height given to the wall in the eleventh century. This band continues, always at the same level, around the two southern and northern wings; we find it again in the north-eastern corner of the façade-wall (J), of which a fragment is preserved.

One can assume that this last course of fourth-century masonry marked the level where the cornice was placed. Hakim's demolishers seemingly ceased their efforts at this point, having thrown down the sculpted stones. Normally, the exterior and interior cornices would be on the same level, as one can see, for example, in the Pantheon in Rome, where the internal Corinthian ordering is identical with that of the great peristyle of its principal entrance. If the same had occurred in the case of the Holy Sepulchre, the level of the interior cornice should have corresponded with that suggested by the last upper course of the circular wall.

If we accept this hypothesis, a reconstruction of the interior dimensions would have been possible, based on the plan which we have. But, very fortunately, we have more: it has proved possible to reconstruct one of the columns of the original interior composition, by reference to two of the columns re-erected in the eleventh century. This allows us to fix the almost exact level of the interior cornice and, thereby, to deduce the vertical volume of the edifice.

Columns nos. 2 and 3 did not collapse at the time of the fire of 1808, but were very badly damaged (Pl. XVIII). However, ringed with iron and encased within square pillars, they have been, most fortunately, preserved. In the course of our work, they have been freed and carefully measured. These two columns are not identical; one of them, no. 3, was only the lower part of a column, and a plain plinth was cut at its lower end. On the other hand, at the top of column no. 2, a fillet astragal, with two projections, indicated that it was an upper section (Pl. XIX).

Their diameter and height measurements were as follows:

Column no. 3	*In millimetres*
Diameter at the base plinth	1,170
Diameter above	1,125
Diameter at the top	1,110
Height	3,545
Column no. 2	
Diameter at the base	1,106
Diameter above	1,030
Diameter at the upper band	1,093
Height	3,600

These dimensions would suggest that the two columns, nos. 2 and 3, combined to form but one. Moreover, the surfaces of the lower part of no. 3 and the upper part of no. 2 were striated, more or less similarly, as if scored with a saw. A whole column, which had fallen without breaking, must have been sawn into two equal pieces to make two columns, the one 3·545 metres in length, and the other 3·600 metres. The complete column, including the saw-mark of 5 millimetres, measured 7·15 metres.

The proportions of such a column are, as a point of comparison, nearly the same as those of the columns of Bethlehem. At Bethlehem, for a height of 4·45 metres, the diameter measures 62 cm.; that is to say, the height is 7·18 diameters. In the Holy Sepulchre, for a height of 7·15 metres, the diameter measures 1·2 metres, i.e. the height is 6·38 diameters. The Corinthian style of the Holy Sepulchre was slightly less slender than that of Bethlehem.

The plinth which has been recovered measured 1,775 mm., while the capital, like the one in Bethlehem, must have had the height of one diameter, i.e. 1,120 mm. Therefore, the height of the whole, below the architrave, reached 10·05 metres (1·78 + 7·15 + 1·12 = 10·05). The height at which the cornice was placed above the frieze could, therefore, have been 11·60 metres. The uppermost course of the circular wall is at a height of 11·10 metres, i.e. 50 cm. lower, which would correspond to a course

forming a frieze under the cornice. We thus rediscover the
interior and exterior cornices at the same height. The height of
the principal interior styling is fixed with a minimum of error,
and so it becomes possible to reconstruct, in imagination, the
vertical volume of the whole edifice.

When Arculf speaks of the upper-floor columns, I do not
think that he can be alluding to a gallery, or gynaeceum, from
which women watched the ceremonies. One does not get the
impression that Egeria looked down, from a height of eleven
metres, upon the ceremonies in the Rotunda. The gynaeceum,
where women were burnt during the fire started by the Persians,
could only have been wooden stands, added later to the deambulatory, which was very high and measured 12·10 metres
beneath its roof.

6. *The façade of the Rotunda: the eight doors of Arculf*

The façade-wall was absolutely rectilinear; one can still
follow its traces, from the north-east angle of the northern wing
(J) to the south-east angle of the southern wing (I), in spite of
the substantial modifications which it has undergone. As I have
already shown, the north-east angle (J) is still visible from the
outside up to a height of 11·10 metres, while the south-west
angle, masked by a medieval tower, is visible only from the
inside up to the same height. Between these two points, the
wall was, in the seventh century and again in the eleventh, destroyed and transformed, but its original alignment has not been
changed.

Thus, the springings of the great arch of the eleventh century
are laid along the alignment of the original wall. The emplacement of the doorways of the northern lateral vestibule (X and Y)
has, likewise, remained unchanged, despite the important
changes in the façade brought about by the restoration work of
Modestus, following the Persians' act of arson. It was possible
that, at this period, a small apse was constructed in the axis of
the building, but of this one cannot be too sure. Arculf certainly
talked of an altar opposite the Tomb, to the east; that is to
say, towards the façade. Moreover, such an altar is shown in
the famous sketch in the manuscripts (Fig. 5); but no apse is
shown, the wall being simply incurved.

The façade, modified at its centre, also underwent changes on
both sides by the doorways, above which high arched windows
replaced the original flattened relieving-arches. These archings

are still partially preserved, above the passage arches introduced in the twelfth century. On either side, there are two arcades, together with the beginning of a third one, modified and walled in the eleventh century. These mark the locations of the passage doorways of the southern and northern vestibules (F and G), as they were seen by Arculf.

These arcades are larger than those of the north, which suggests that there was a more radical rearrangement of the

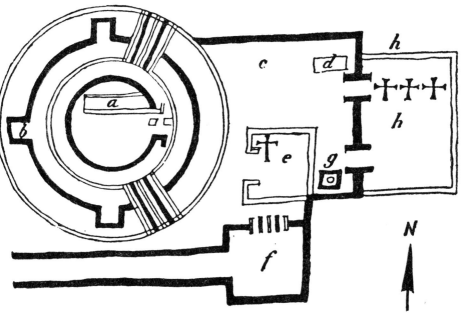

Fig. 5. Arculf's plan of the Holy Sepulchre in the seventh century (*Cod. Parisiensis 13048; ninth century*)

southern side of the façade (Z) in the seventh century, while the arrangement of the passage doorways of the northern lateral vestibule (X and Y) was retained. The springings of the archways are, indeed, supported on the pillars which separated the original doorways. Two of these pillars remain, up to the level of the original door-lintels (X and Y). The place of a third pillar, destroyed in the twelfth century, is indicated by the springing of the two archways of Modestus. Thus, the emplacement of the three original doorways of the northern vestibule is ascertained.

One of the pillars between the two doorways (X) is fairly well preserved. The grooving of the southern face of the door-jamb remains, the level of one lintel is certain, while the grooving of the northern face of the jamb was refashioned in the twelfth century, but remains very visible (Pl. XX*a*). Why, then, in these circumstances, does Arculf talk of eight doors? We have recognized three on the north side and, on the southern side, there were, likewise, three. The missing doors were, probably, placed in the archways opening on to the southern and northern porticos of the courtyard.

On the pillar between X and Y, which was destroyed in the twelfth century, rested a large archway, of which the springer can still be seen on the lateral face of point M. This archway, spanning the width of the lateral vestibules, joined the façade-wall to the masonry of the central cylindrical area, having, therefore, an important stabilizing effect. But its very presence made the reinforcing of the façade-wall absolutely necessary, to offset the oblique thrust which it imposed. This reinforcement of the wall, following the reconstruction of Modestus, was achieved by pilasters fixed against the ancient wall.

The façade of the fourth century may have been reinforced by a peristyle of eight columns. Were these engaged columns, placed against the façade-wall, or were they disengaged columns, whose axis would have been 2·30 metres away from the façade? The hypothesis of a peristyle of eight columns is admissible; its composite style would have been identical to that of the interior, with its columns of 7·15 metres in height. The intercolumniation is indicated by the spacing of the pillars between the doorways of the lateral vestibules. The doors of the southern vestibule, as modified by Modestus, were originally symmetrical with those of the northern side; thus, the intercolumniation would have been 3·30 metres, making 23·10 metres altogether, which is the same as the exterior diameter of the Rotunda; so far, so good.

But the foundations of the façade-wall have been unearthed at point Z, and there is no trace of any foundations of an engaged column backing on to the façade. The foundation-wall measures from 1·45 to 1·60 metres, while the façade-wall measured 1·42 metres. Another foundation-wall, which, itself, could also date from the fourth century, was exposed in 1961, 1·7 metres in front of the façade-wall, i.e. to the east. This measured 1·20 metres in width, and could have served as the foundation for the columns of a peristyle, whose axis would have been 2·30 metres from the façade-wall. But, to the right of point Z, the foundation-wall no longer exists and, on the north side, it has not been rediscovered.

What, then, can we conclude? It would seem probable that the façade of the Rotunda included a peristyle of eight columns with a pediment; it would have had a width equal to the cylindrical volume of the Rotunda and the axis of its columns would have been 2·30 metres from the wall of the façade. But the foundations were destroyed during the work of the twelfth century, with the exception of the piece excavated in 1961.

7. *The form of the Rotunda*

To conclude this study of the Rotunda, I should emphasise what gives it its special character. It is clearly not an arrange-

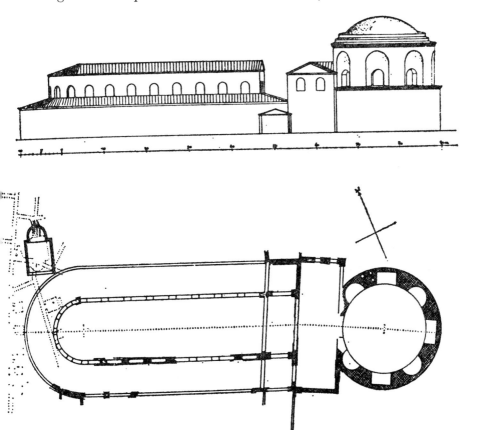

Fig. 6. Mausoleum of the Empress Helena in the Basilica of SS. Peter and Marcellinus, Rome (*After Deichmann and Tschira, J.d.I., 72, 49, fig. 5*)

ment *a posteriori*; set up over the Tomb of the Lord, to exalt the glory of His Resurrection, it expresses an idea of Triumph. The Rotunda is a monument to the glory of Christ the Conqueror.

Its round shape, it should be noted, is the same as that of the great Roman mausoleums. Would it be an irreverence to draw a parallel between the Holy Sepulchre and the Tower of Herodium? In the latter, one can see a certain similarity of form, where the rectilinear façade-wall is also tangential to the circular volume of the Tower, which looks like a mausoleum.[1] The mausoleum of the Empress Helena in Rome (Fig. 6) was also a tower attached to a rectilinear vestibule.[2]

What differentiates the Holy Sepulchre from the Roman mausoleums is the delicacy of the masonry supporting the former; the vaulting of the Mausoleums of St. Helena or St. Constantia entailed very thick walls. The Rotunda was a mausoleum, but large crowds had to move around within it. Since vaulting was replaced by wooden ceilings or timbered roofing, heavy walls became unnecessary. The basic supports are lightly poised, while the lateral vestibules are very open, thus giving the impression of free circulation in a large, semi-circular space. But the central area, the Rotunda itself, retains something of the majesty that characterizes great circular spaces, such as that of the Pantheon of Agrippa in Rome.

One can well believe that, in Constantine's thoughts, the Rotunda was the triumphal mausoleum erected to the memory of the Risen One, the founder of the Church. As the cities of ancient Greece erected 'heroa' to the memory of their founders, so the Emperor had a 'heröon' raised over the Tomb of the Lord, to the glory of the founder of the New Jerusalem; in the same manner, he had his own erected over his tomb in Constantinople, the New Rome. This thought of Monsieur Grabar[3] seems to me worthy of the grandeur of the monument which our work has permitted us to discover.

[1] Fr. V. Corbo, 'L'Herodion di Giabal Fureidis', *L.A.* (xvii) 1967.
[2] Friedrich Wilhelm Deichmann, 'Das Mausoleum der Kaiserin Helena', *J.D.A.I.* 1957, pp. 44 ff.
[3] André Grabar, *Martyrium*, pp. 257 ff.

III

CONSTANTINE'S BASILICA AND GOLGOTHA

So far, the fourth-century features which have been preserved within and around the Rotunda have allowed us to attempt a reconstruction in which there has perhaps been a modicum of imagination. But there is a curb to our imagination—those great walls, still standing—to prevent it from running wild.

When we now turn to a study of the Basilica of Constantine, we do not have such reliable witnesses. Completely destroyed by Hakim at the beginning of the eleventh century, few vestiges have survived, and their interpretation must remain somewhat conjectural. One very important event, however, has occurred, bringing much light with it. In 1968, the foundations of the western apse of the Basilica were uncovered by my colleague Athanase Ekonomopoulos, thus fixing, quite certainly, the emplacement of the whole edifice (Pl. XX*b*).

By tradition, the Rotunda is called by its Greek name of *Anastasis* or *Resurrection*. If the name 'Rotunda' is less uplifting, it is, nevertheless, more current in everyday language. Furthermore, it creates a picture, evoking, in itself, a circular building and, for this reason, I have adopted it. Moreover, Arculf and many others employed this name long before myself.

This question of nomenclature also arises in the case of the Martyrium. Arculf has already said: 'There is joined to the eastern side of the church built over the site of Calvary, the basilica so magnificently constructed by King Constantine, which is called the Martyrium.' But, today, this name can lead to confusion, since it formerly designated the church of the Cross adjacent to Golgotha. For latinists, the word 'martyr' evokes thoughts of suffering; but the Greek word 'marturion' implies, rather, the idea of witnessing: it would be a holy place which bore witness.[1] Thus, for Eusebius of Caesarea, the 'marturion' was all the holy places which, together, had witnessed the providential history of salvation; it was just as much the empty Tomb, as it was Golgotha. I prefer, therefore, to use the expression, 'the Basilica of Constantine'. It is still none the less true

---

[1] André Grabar, op. cit., p. 29.

that, from the time of Egeria to the time of Arculf, the expression 'Martyrium' has, by tradition, referred to the Basilica, which was the major church of Jerusalem. Later, however, Arab chroniclers spoke also of 'St. Constantine', 'Mar Constantin'.

At the beginning, in the year 333, the Pilgrim of Bordeaux himself also spoke only of a basilica. Near Golgotha, he tells us, 'a basilica was built at the command of Constantine, that is to say, a church, of wonderful beauty'. The detailed description that Eusebius has given of it will greatly help us to rediscover how it might have looked.

The problem more difficult to resolve will be that of the church of Golgotha, of which Arculf spoke, while the Pilgrim of Bordeaux mentioned only 'the little hill of Golgotha'. It is true that this church could be later than the restoration made by Modestus, but of this we cannot be too sure, since Egeria herself speaks of the ceremonies which took place at Golgotha on Good Friday.

1. *The courtyard in front of the Rotunda and the rock of Calvary*

One may wonder why Egeria called the courtyard situated between the Rotunda and the Basilica of Constantine 'parvis ante crucem'; that is to say, 'in front of the Cross'. It would have been more logical to talk of 'the forecourt of the Rotunda', since all the doors of the sanctuary opened on to this courtyard, where the faithful assembled, beneath the porticos, before cock-crow, to await their opening. Previously, before the construction of the Rotunda and its façade, the same courtyard stretched westward and continued around the Tomb. I have already examined this question.

Eusebius, who described the courtyard as being 'decorated with a stone paving and surrounded on three sides by long porticos', goes on to say that 'the side directly facing the grotto, that is to say, the eastern side, was closed by the Basilica, rising to a considerable height'.

The foundations of the apse, and of the portico at the back of it, having been excavated, together with those of the lateral porticos, their emplacement is now known exactly. Two porticos bounded the courtyard, one to the south, the other to the north. The third lay to the east, against the great eastern wall of the Basilica, into which the apse was inserted.

This eastern portico abutted on the rock of Calvary, of which Eusebius does not, unfortunately, speak. The mantle of dressed masonry, in which the rock was enclosed, must have merged with the architecture of the porticos. Were they, therefore, already constructed, and was the courtyard already laid out, when the Pilgrim of Bordeaux came there? Golgotha appeared to him to be a 'hillock', which does not conjure up a particular vision of architecture. Later, there was mention of a large Cross surmounting Calvary, hence the name of the 'parvis ante crucem'. The architectural arrangement of all this is difficult to envisage.

It would seem probable that the summit of the rock, at the spot where it had been slotted to support the Cross, was venerated from the Basilica, whose ground level was very much higher than that of the courtyard. It must have been very near the existing level of the Canons' cloister. It cannot have been until after the seventh century, and almost certainly in the eleventh, that the rock of Calvary was worshipped from the western side.

What, we ask ourselves, is the rock of Calvary really like? It has never been systematically studied. It is almost completely enclosed inside the existing monument, and it would be necessary to disengage it completely in order to understand it better. However, some indications have been collected as a result of the excavations of 1961.

In Adam's Chapel, that is to say to the west of the rock, there is, at a depth of more than five metres, a quarry bed. A confusion of disused columns, piled up as foundations by the Crusaders, prevent one descending. On the northern side, a blockage of stones in the Byzantine earth-fill likewise prevents descent. But boring-rods have been inserted for more than five metres in depth. Under the forecourt, some metres to the south of Calvary, the bottom of the large cistern is 6·75 metres deep; I do not know the level of the rock to the east.

Based on these observations, it would seem that the rock of Calvary is a vertical block, which must have remained isolated, in the corner of an ancient quarry. From top to bottom, it measures between ten and eleven metres. A cavern situated under the existing façade of the church, and which communicates with the cistern, still at 6·75 metres depth, could, in relation to the vertical block, have been a tomb.

From this, could we not put forward the hypothesis that the vertical block was the 'nephesh' of a hellenistic tomb, similar to those at Kidron?[1] The ancient quarry, from which it was cut,

[1] N. Avigad, *Ancient Monuments in the Kidron Valley* (1954), and André Parrot, *Golgotha*, p. 64

was filled in by the time of Christ; the earth accumulated around the 'nephesh' formed a mound, from out of the top of which emerged the tip of the bare and rounded rock, like a skull-cap: this was Golgotha. A stone's throw away, the tomb of Joseph of Arimathea was cut into a vertical rock face belonging to the same quarry, whose bed rose in terraces from east to west, while the olive trees of the garden grew out of the earth used to fill in the ancient quarry. There is no connection between the hypothesis proposed here and the legend which insisted that Adam's tomb was situated at Golgotha.[1]

In the second century, mystic speculation, born of the Judaeo-Christian milieu of Jerusalem, had transferred the Jewish legend of the tomb of Adam at Mount Moriah from the altar of the Temple to Golgotha. Origen knew of this tradition, which is not far removed from the thinking of St. Paul, who saw in Christ the 'New Adam', taking the place of the former to make amends for the Original Sin[2]. This train of thought is earlier than the excavations of the fourth century and the fervour that those provoked.

At that time, men sought to explain the name 'Golgotha' on the basis of the legend of Adam's tomb. Golgotha was simply the 'place of the skull' of Adam, without reference to any sort of supporting discovery. All this existed only on a level of pure speculation, bathing itself in the sunlight of the theory of 'Christ the Last Adam'.

However, this idea of Golgotha as the place of the skull of Adam, which lent itself to enriching spiritual consequences, pleased the Fathers of the Church. One finds it in St. Cyril of Jerusalem, St. Epiphanius of Salamine, St. Basil of Caesarea, and in many others. St. Jerome preferred to explain the name 'Golgotha', in a more down-to-earth sense, as a 'rounded rock' in the shape of a skull, while his penitents, Paula and Eustochium, supported the reference to Adam's skull.

The legend of Adam's Tomb at Golgotha was totally unknown to the Evangelists. When they speak of the place called 'of the skull', in Hebrew 'Golgotha', they are using popular language, which likes names that conjure up pictures; thus they call a rounded rock 'the skull'. But, in any case, the origin of the name 'Golgotha' can only be a matter of speculation, for there is no solid foundation for an unchallengeable interpretation.

---

[1] J. Jeremias, *Golgotha*.
[2] Rom. 5 : 12 ff.

2. *The Basilica*

To the east of the courtyard, with its three porticos, the chevet of the Basilica of Constantine 'rises to a considerable height'. One would think that, since the Rotunda was more or less in the axis of the western side of the courtyard, the apse of the Basilica should have been along the axis of the eastern side, but the foundations of the apse, having been discovered, have provided proof this this was not so. Brought to light under the choir of the Katholicon, they are, in relation to the axis of the present apse, and, likewise, in relation to the axis of the Rotunda, completely offset towards the south. It follows from this that the apse was contiguous to the rock of Calvary.

Its position determines that of the central nave. We know from Eusebius, that 'the multitude of the faithful, who entered from outside, came in by three doorways, well placed on the east of the building. In front of the doorways, at the extreme western end of the Basilica, was the apse.' It was the foundations of this apse, which 'crowned the whole edifice', that my colleague Athanase Ekonomopoulos presented to the public on 2 March 1971.[1]

It happens that the longitudinal axis of the crypt of St. Helena, if followed to the west, coincides with the axis of the apse. Thus, the lateral walls of the crypt would be the foundations that had been preserved from the lateral colonnades of the nave (Pl. XXI); its width, of the order of 13·50 metres, would have been a very reasonable dimension. By comparison, the nave of the Basilica of St. Peter, built in Rome on Constantine's orders, shortly after the Basilica of Jerusalem, measures 24·00 metres, while that of Bethlehem a little less than 10·00 metres only.

The existing crypt of St. Helena was constructed in the twelfth century, and only the lateral walls are earlier. It seems probable that the Basilica of Constantine had no crypt. Steps, and a vaulted passage along the southern lateral wall, led to the grotto of the Cross. The paving of the Basilica rested on rubble, which was confirmed by the test borings that were made beyond the apses. Remains of the walls supporting the vaults, which would have been necessary if a crypt had existed, have not been found. Are the existing lateral walls to be dated as being of the fourth century, or are they earlier?

Some indications make one think that certain parts of the

---

[1] *Jerusalem Post*, 3 March 1971.

northern wall, which goes down to bedrock beneath the rubble, are of the time of Hadrian. If this is so, the Basilica of Constantine would be a transformation of the civic basilica of Hadrian, whose central nave could have measured 19·00 by 40·00 metres without an apse. Then, only the lateral southern wall would be of the fourth century. The location of the rock of Calvary, disengaged only by Constantine's work, would have determined the width of the nave and the emplacement of the apse. All this, however, remains to be verified.

The width of the nave is, therefore, determined by that of the crypt. 'On the one and the other of its flanks', Eusebius tells us, 'twin, double-porticoed, upper and lower galleries, with gilded ceilings, ran parallel to each other. The front row consisted of columns of large dimension, while the row behind was formed of square pillars, richly decorated on their surfaces.' It is not necessary to clarify this description; as in Bethlehem or in St. Peter's in Rome, it was a basilica with five naves. Its special particularity was that it had an upper storey. A row of square pillars, and probably arcades, served as intermediate supports for the floor-boards. The width of the lateral naves still remains indicated on the ground by lines of equidistant walls, which are parallel to the walls of the crypt of St. Helena.

On the southern side, the foundations of the intermediate supports have been rediscovered in a Greek quarter, to the east of Calvary, while the external wall is identifiable, for a length of 15·00 metres, in the Chapel of the Ethiopians.

The rock of Calvary was situated in the axis of the first southern lateral nave, while the other nave must have opened on to a passage leading to the Rotunda. An arcade, which appears to be of the fourth century, at the end of the Greek refectory, opened towards Calvary; another arcade returned to the northern face of Calvary. It would seem that, given these conditions, a ciborium of four arches covered the summit of the rock, which one reached by going through the Basilica; the four existing arches of the Chapel of the Calvary would have been a part of that ancient ciborium.

On the northern side, more recent walls have been built on the ancient foundations, thus indicating their emplacement. The existing street, which serves the Coptic convent, would have been one of the northern lateral naves. The façade-wall of this convent is erected on the foundations of the outer northern wall, while the wall enclosing the courtyard of the Ethiopians rests on the ancient foundations of the intermediate supports.

The eastern façade-wall of the Basilica is more difficult to determine. However, I believe that one can make it coincide with the wall that encloses the garden of the Ethiopians from the street. Its alignment was not perpendicular to that of the five naves, the façade-wall being at a slant in relation to the lateral walls, its south-eastern angle being acute and its north-eastern one obtuse. This deformation must have been originally intended, in order to seek equilibrium with the shape of the entrance courtyard.

The façade of the Basilica and the alignment of the Cardo Maximus were each slanted, but in opposite directions. Thus, the interior space of the courtyard took the form of an isosceles trapezium. The three doorways leading into the Basilica, and which Eusebius judged to be 'well placed', opened on to this courtyard; that is to say, on to the atrium. Therefore, owing to the foundation alignments which have been reused, the Basilica with its five naves, as described by Eusebius, is fairly easy to reindicate on the ground it occupied, around the crypt of St. Helena.

Up till now, I have spoken only of the siting and of the general form of the building. But Eusebius's description is very much more complete and will help lift the wings of your imagination:

The interior surface of the building [he says] was hidden under slabs of multi-coloured marble. The exterior aspect of the walls, embellished with well-matched and polished stones, gave an effect of extraordinary beauty, which yielded nothing to the appearance of the marble. As to its roofing, the outside was covered with lead, a sure protection against the winter rains; the inside of the roof was decorated with sculpted coffering, which, like some great ocean, covered the whole Basilica with its endless swell, while the brilliant gold with which it was covered, made the whole temple sparkle with a thousand reflections.

Thus may your imagination take flight; do not forget that Constantine desired that this church should be worthy 'of his wealth and of his crown'.

Is it possible for us to determine the height of the colonnades of the lateral naves, and that of the ground-floor and of the upper floor? The dimensions of the Byzantine columns, re-utilized during the works of the eleventh century, can give us some indication. Those of the Arches of the Virgin measure between 3·75 metres and 3·90 metres; they are about 0·57 metres in diameter. In the Katholikon, near Calvary, a reused column from the twelfth century is smaller, measuring 3·55 metres. On the upper floor of the Rotunda, the two columns on either side of the great archway measure 3·62 metres, with a diameter of 0·52 metres. Others, in the medieval gallery of the northern transept, are even smaller, being 2·75 metres. One can make no assumptions concerning such diverse measurements, except, perhaps, that they probably did not come from the Basilica. However, one of them had a dimension which could have suited the colonnade of the first storey. It is that of the Katholikon, with its height of 3·55 metres and its diameter of 0·50 metres. But 3·62 metres and a diameter of 0·52 metres would also have been reasonable dimensions. The ground-floor colonnade could have been 4·80 metres in height, which would have harmonized with the 7·15 metres of the columns of the Rotunda.

It is most probable that the central nave was lit by high windows. The roofing of the lateral naves, owing to the first storey, necessitated the placing of windows at quite a height, which resulted in an interior space of essentially vertical proportions. This would explain the words of Eusebius, who saw the apse of the Basilica rising to a 'considerable height'. The nave must have measured some 22 metres from floor to ceiling.

In my exposé, I have assumed that, at the western end of the Basilica, there was an apse. The term used by Eusebius can be transcribed as 'hemispheriou'. Father Abel found this word inexplicable. In general terms, we think it describes an apse, although the word makes one think, rather, of a cupola. The problem is further complicated by reason of 'the twelve columns engirdling the apse, equal in number to the Apostles of the Saviour, which were decorated at their summit with great silver urns, an offering of splendour rendered by the Emperor to his God'. The twelve columns are, indeed, very crowded in their apse. Professor Krautheimer has suggested the solution of a horseshoe-shaped apse, which would have given more space. It has not been possible to determine very precisely the exact emplacement of the chevet-wall of the Basilica, through which the apse extended. The solution to this problem could be found if the location of this chevet-wall could be more exactly identified.

3. *The atrium and the propylaea*

'Those emerging from the Basilica by the eastern gateways', Eusebius goes on to say, 'came upon another open space where, in a first atrium, exedrae had been placed, round and about.

Beyond, on the public highway, were the propylaea serving the whole building, whose artistic arrangement offered to the passers-by a foretaste of what they would see inside.' All of this monumental entrance has, fortunately, not been lost; the three doorways of the atrium have been preserved, and two of them are still to be seen, one in an annexe of the church of the Alexander Hospice, the other in the shop of Zalatimos, the pastrycook.

Father Vincent has made a detailed study of them.[1] The one in the Alexander Hospice was the southernmost door; to accommodate it, an opening was cut in a large existing wall. The door in the pastrycook's shop was the central one, and its jambs were made by very carefully refashioning the masonry work in the old wall (Pl. XXIIa). Being in the axis of the Basilica, its position is of great importance. Thanks to this fact, we are able to verify that the axis of the apse, that of the crypt of St. Helena, and the axis of the central doorway are in a straight line. Thus, the axis of the whole building is known over a length of 75·00 metres, and its position, therefore, definitely established. One may regret that this principal door is not better displayed, for it is a precious witness of the history of the Holy Sepulchre. The gate 'of Ephraim' so-called, together with its threshold, would, likewise, have been a modification made to the fourth-century wall. On the other hand, the fitting of the angle contiguous to it can be neither a transformation nor a reconstruction, it is an ancient piece of work.

The southern wall of the atrium, joining it, is evidently of later date; it is a pilastered wall, perpendicular to the large wall in which the gateways were inserted. Its alignment being different to that of the walls of the Basilica, one may believe that it is not of the fourth century. It must have been conserved and merely reused, since it was well placed to be a wall of the atrium. It would have been part of Hadrian's works, while the large wall and its angle are earlier. The pilastered wall would have been joined to a Herodian feature, probably an element of the southern face of the terrace, on which the civic basilica of Aelia Capitolina was constructed.

The three entry gateways of the atrium are very well indicated on the mosaic of Madaba, where they are the principal feature of the façade, in front of which the porticos of the Cardo Maximus cease, the better to allow it to stand out. Must we conclude from this, that the propylaea were only a long flight

---

[1] Fr. Vincent, *Jér. nouv.*, chap. II.

of steps leading back from the street-line? It is certain that, without the porticos, the indication of the mosaicist lends much grandeur to the entrance. This recessing is, in itself, most imposing, and a screen of columns would have quite spoiled its effect. I think it is quite unnecessary to add anything to the façade as it is here presented.

'In the atrium, exedrae were placed round and about.' Does this mean at each end of the narthex, or scattered about in different places? For my part, I would imagine a group of recesses on the north side of the atrium. As for the narthex, this could have been an arcaded portico, allowing a greater height along the façade.

4. The buildings around the Basilica: the Baptistry

We have already seen that to the north of the Rotunda there were several monastic cells, arranged around a courtyard. Similar dependent buildings must have existed around the Basilica; the dwelling of the Bishop, which would later become known as the Patriarchate, must certainly have formed a part of these annexes of the church. A careful study of the plan of Jerusalem on the Madaba mosaic, together with other documents, where place-names are given, has enabled us to establish maps of the city in Byzantine times,[1] which show the location of its principal buildings. To the north of the four features making up the Holy Sepulchre, that is to say the entrance atrium, the Basilica, the atrium of the Rotunda, and the Rotunda itself, all are agreed on the location of the Patriarchate and another monastery; to the south, there would have been the agora and the baptistry.

The Madaba plan shows, to the north of the Rotunda, a red parallelogram, which is believed to represent a religious building. Some have thought to see there the location of the monastery of the Anastasis, where there had been loss of life during the fire started by the Persians. The validity of this interpretation is corroborated by the existence of the monastic cells and the courtyard, which have been identified to the north of the Rotunda, and which lend plausibility to these interpreters of the plan. In their opinion, the Patriarchate is represented by the yellow and brown triangle shown to the north of the

[1] Michael Avi-Yonah, *Madaba Mosaïc Map* (1954); J. T. Milik, 'Topographie de Jérusalem', *Mélanges de l'Université Saint-Joseph*, vol. xxxvii, Fasc. 7 (Beirut, 1961).

entrance, and it is probable that the Bishop's dwelling occupied the whole area to the north of the Basilica.

In this same area a large wall, that can be followed along a stretch of nearly 60 metres, could have been the northern limit of the public domain, occupied by the Hadrianic city centre; that is to say, the Forum, the Temple, and the Basilica. Constantine's town-plan would have been carried out in this public part, while the dwelling of the Bishop would have backed on to the large wall. The courtyard, larger than the others, running the length of the Basilica, could have been a garden. The storey above the lateral naves must have involved the existence of important staircases. I have adopted the solution of double flights of exterior stairways in the courtyards, along the lateral façades.

To the south of the picture of the Holy Sepulchre, the mosaicist of Madaba indicated, behind the porticos, a brown patch to the left of the entrance and, close to the Rotunda, a red lozenge divided into four parts. The interpreters have called these two features respectively the agora, or market, and the baptistry. The agora evidently occupied the site of the ancient forum of Hadrian, the monumental entrance of which faced the Cardo Maximus. A pilaster, still preserved in the Alexander Hospice, adorned the north-west corner, which helps to establish its approximate emplacement. If Constantine's building operations had not preserved this monumental entrance, nothing would remain, and everything would have been entirely removed. One may, therefore, assume that the triple gateway of Hadrian was still in use after the construction of the Basilica; it was, perhaps, the Persians who tore it down. A reconstruction of Hadrian's archways would fix the axis of the Roman town-plan, which could only have been perpendicular to the direction of the Cardo Maximus; that is to say, parallel to the pilastered wall in the Alexander Hospice.

An important piece of masonry, measuring 34·00 metres in length and more than 3·00 metres in thickness, still exists in the area. It was reused, in the twelfth century, as the southern wall of the Canons' refectory, its alignment being parallel to that of the axis of the forum. It follows from this, that the origin of this mass is probably to be sought in a monumental architectural feature; for example, it could have been the façade, with its niches, of a double staircase giving access to the terraces. Such a feature could well have been retained because of its decorative aspect and, because it did not interfere with the layout of the

Basilica, it would also have contributed to demarcating the church territory.

A little further to the west, the emplacement of a doorway was discovered, in 1964, in a wall running east–west, in the middle of the existing entry forecourt; its masonry-work and the nearby paving are of the fourth century. This doorway was a secondary entrance to the forecourt of the Rotunda, while the wall also marked the southern boundary of the church area, rejoining the angle of the great Roman wall of which I have just spoken.

As for the location of the baptistry, at the far end of the ancient forum, to the south of the Rotunda, we have, on the whole, to rely on the testimony of the Pilgrim of Bordeaux to recognize it in the red lozenge of the Madaba plan. The reference in the text is as follows: 'At the side of the Basilica, there are reservoirs from where water is raised, and behind [*a tergo*], a baptistry where children are purified [*balneum ubi infantes lavantur*].' All this must, evidently, have been to the south of the Basilica, since the Pilgrim saw Golgotha on his left, the Grotto a stone's throw away and, near Golgotha, the Basilica. He is in the forum, which he is crossing from west to east. He leaves the baptistry behind him and sees, on the southern side of the Basilica, reservoirs 'from which water is raised'. Since one does not raise water from a spring but, rather, from a well or a cistern, these reservoirs, of which he speaks, are evidently the large cisterns which are still in existence; that of Hadrian's time is underneath the forum, and the Byzantine cistern is underneath the existing forecourt.

The location of the baptistry is, probably, to be found in the complex of chapels to the west of the present-day forecourt. No confirmation has been sought as to whether there is any ancient masonry under these chapels; the masonry-work, as a whole, dates from the eleventh century, partially modified in the twelfth by the construction of the tower. It is noteworthy that the Pilgrim of Bordeaux, who does not speak of the Rotunda, nevertheless saw the baptistry behind Constantine's Basilica. It must, therefore, have been in use before the completion of the Rotunda. Was it, then, a Roman building put to another use; for example, as the hall of a thermal Bath-house, whence the expression 'balneum' used to describe it? Its utilization from the year 333 onwards would support such a suggestion. In so far as the chapels of the eleventh century have kept something of their original design, their partition into three elements is well suited to a baptistry.

Addressing himself to those recently baptized at the first mystagogic religious class, St. Cyril (A.D. 350) or his successor, John of Jerusalem (387–417), expressed himself thus: 'First, you entered the vestibule of the baptistry. . . . Standing, turned to the west, you have heard. . . . ' The Bishop was here talking of the rite of Renunciation. In a first room, which faced the west, the candidate for baptism renounced Satan; then, stripped of his tunic, he was led by the hand, 'to the holy pool of divine baptism', situated in a second room. He then entered the water, with his face to the east. The baptismal cistern was hollowed out of the ground, and he descended into it by steps.[1] On coming out of the water, the baptised received in a third room the white robe of his new and stainless birth.

The three rooms, with a passage uniting them, are still quite traceable in the existing layout. The left-hand room was the vestibule, by which one entered and faced west to make one's renunciation; the central room was the baptistry proper, where, coming from the passageway, one descended into the water, while one faced the east; in the right-hand room, on the side of the Rotunda, the baptized received his white robe. All this remains to be verified, but it is probable that the pool, dug out of the earth, could be rediscovered.

Egeria does not speak of the baptistry, but notes only that, 'the baptized, on emerging from the font, are clothed in white and are led, together with the Bishop, first of all to the Anastasis . . ., after which he accompanies them to the principal church.' One must conclude from this, that the baptistry was alongside the Rotunda. The place where we locate it corresponds to the proximity suggested by Egeria's liturgical note; I do not think that the baptistry could have been located in the northern courtyard.

Clearly, the large ornamental scroll at the cistern of St. Helena, underneath the northern courtyard, upon which the third verse of the 29th Psalm, 'The voice of the Lord upon the waters', is inscribed, makes one think of a baptismal use for its water. Moreover, it was entered by a large flight of steps, 1·30 metres wide, which led to the bottom, along the length of the semicircular rock-wall. Despite this, I cannot find any place for the location of a baptistry in the northern courtyard, which was a place dedicated to monastic silence and quite isolated.

[1] J. W. Crowfoot, *Early Churches in Palestine*, Schweich Lectures, 1937, p. 55; B. Bagatti, 'I battisteri della Palestina', *Actes du Vᵉ Congrès international d'Archéologie chrétienne*, Aix-en-Provence, 1954; A. Katchatrian, *Les Baptistères paléo-chrétiens* (Paris, 1952), École pratique des Hautes Études, section des Sciences religieuses.

On the other hand, if the baptistry was on the southern side, it would have been accessible from the outside. The baptismal cistern, found in the narthex of the chapel of St. Mary, is of a later period. It would conform better to a baptistry of the eleventh century, or even, perhaps, of the seventh, if one can agree that there was a first arrangement of St. Mary's chapel at the time of the work done by Modestus, as Arculf's text suggests. This states that 'a square church, dedicated to St. Mary, the Mother of God, was joined to the right of the Anastasis': but, 'to the right'—would that be to the north? Perhaps so, since it is on the right when one faces the Tomb.

5. *The church of Golgotha*

It is not easy to imagine the architectural arrangement of the rock of Calvary, which stood at the extreme south of the eastern portico on the forecourt of the Rotunda. All that we know for certain is that the foundations of the colonnade and those of the backwall abut against the rock-mass. It is probable, however, that a chapel was fitted into the corner of the forecourt, even before the seventh century, since 'the Chapel of the Skull', that is to say the skull of Adam, is mentioned in many texts. In any case, it certainly existed after the work of Modestus, who at the same time had a kind of tower set up above the ciborium of Calvary, where today the chapel of Melchisedech is to be found.

At the end of the fourth century, Egeria spoke only of a Cross, raised above Calvary and dominating the courtyard. It would seem that originally there was nothing on the existing site of Adam's chapel, except perhaps a deep recess facing west, which gave a view of the rock. Around the year 350, St. Cyril proclaimed, in one of his religious instructions, 'He will convince Thee, this St. Golgotha, he who dominates and is always to be seen, showing, even unto this day, that the rocks were riven because of Christ'; therefore, one saw the rock then as one sees it today.

But this is not our problem; what we have to resolve is the question of the church of Golgotha. Did there, originally, exist a church of Golgotha separately from that of Constantine's Basilica? In the texts, the Basilica is frequently called the church of Golgotha; even Egeria used it in a stereotyped form, like a refrain repeating itself: 'One betakes oneself to the great church built by Constantine, this church is at Golgotha, behind the Cross.' The rock of Calvary, and the ciborium which capped it, stood at the end of the first nave, on the southern side of the Basilica and so were part of it; for this reason, the Basilica could be called the church of Golgotha. Egeria goes on to say, 'It is called the martyrium, because it is at Golgotha, that is to say behind the Cross, where Our Lord suffered his passion', and, she adds, 'hence the name martyrium', which is a misconstruction, as has already been shown.

However, in one passage alone, Egeria does draw a distinction between the 'martyrium' and another place, which was also 'Behind the Cross'; on Holy Thursday, 'after the dismissal at the Martyrium, they go Behind the Cross . . .; then the Bishop makes the Offering there, and everyone receives Communion. On this one day the Offering is made Behind the Cross, but on no other day in the whole year.'

On the morning of Good Friday, the veneration of the relic of the Cross also took place, she tells us, on the same spot: 'The Bishop's chair is placed on Golgotha Behind the Cross (the cross there now), and he takes his seat. A table is placed before him . . . and there is brought to him a gold and silver box containing the holy Wood of the Cross. . . .' After that, the people filed past, 'entering by one door and going out through the other, till midday. All this takes place where on the previous day, Thursday, they made the Offering.'[1]

Two distinctive points emerge from these texts: there would have been a first place behind the Cross, but still a part of the Basilica, in the prolongation of the lateral nave; in another place, also behind the Cross, but, however, outside the Basilica, the Bishop made the Offering on Holy Thursday and presided over the veneration of the relic of the true Cross, on the morning of Good Friday. It was, truly, a church, where ceremonies could take place and which was enclosed by doors. The space of 4·00 by 4·00 metres, between the top of Calvary and the lateral nave, would seem to me to be too small; it was only a passageway, while the altar for the Offering would have also taken up some space. A square area to the south of Calvary, one at least of whose walls is of the fourth century, could be the remains of that church. Within the general plan of the Basilica, the church of Golgotha could have extended to the south of Calvary, along the prolongation of the southern lateral nave, which allowed for movement. It would have had direct access from the secondary atrium, which, to the south, preceded the forecourt of the Rotunda.

[1] The Revd. John Wilkinson, *Egeria's Travels* (S.P.C.K., London, 1972), pp. 134–5, 136–7.

This hypothesis would help to explain Arculf's text, which poses some difficulties; having described the Tomb in great detail, he again speaks of the Rotunda: 'this round church . . . bears the name of Anastasis; that is to say, Resurrection. To the right, the square church of St. Mary is joined to it. . . . Another very large church, facing east, has been built on the spot called, in Hebrew, Golgotha. . . .' At first sight, one might think that Arculf was here referring to the Basilica of Constantine; but not at all, for he goes on to add: 'To this church, made of blocks of dressed stone and built on the place of Calvary, is joined on the eastern side, the Basilica so magnificently constructed by King Constantine, and which is called the Martyrium.'

Thus, there are two churches: the Basilica of Constantine, clearly identified, and 'another very large church facing east'. One can assume that its apse was to the east and its entrance to the west, while the Basilica was in the opposite alignment, with its apse to the west and its entrance to the east. The expression 'large church' excludes the possibility that Arculf was talking of the extremity of the lateral nave. A little further on, he adds: 'Between the Basilica of Golgotha and the Martyrium, there is an exedra, in which the chalice of the Lord is displayed, the same one that he blessed with his own hand during the Last Supper. . . .' This exedra near Calvary could be precisely that small-sized extremity of the lateral nave, but then a further difficulty would arise, since Arculf goes on to say: 'In this same church [of Golgotha], there is a grotto hollowed out of the rock under the place of the Cross of the Lord. . . .' This evidently refers to the chapel 'of the skull', which, according to my plan, would not have been beneath the church of Golgotha, but alongside it.

I think one can allow that, here, there is nothing more than an imprecision, which would, anyhow, be contradicted by the diagram accompanying the manuscripts. The square area to the south, and its long corridor running westward, would be the Basilica of Golgotha, the light-coloured square alongside would be Calvary and 'the Skull', while the long corridor would be the secondary atrium.

Before closing this study, I would like to give an explanation for the slanted insertion of the northern portico of the forecourt of the Rotunda; for this, I shall once again have recourse to Arculf. His plan indicates a rectangle in the north-eastern corner of the forecourt, which would be an offertory table, connected with the place of Abraham's sacrifice. I have already dealt with the question of the transfer, even earlier than the fourth century, of the sites of the tomb of Adam and of Abraham's sacrifice from the Temple to Golgotha. At the time this work was carried out, the transfer was, already, an intellectual *fait accompli*. The sacrifice of Isaac, symbolic of Christ's own sacrifice, could not have happened anywhere other than at Golgotha, or nearby. Therefore, the location would then have been fixed at the north-eastern corner of the forecourt, facing Golgotha. This was a sufficient reason for inserting, slantwise, the northern portico of the forecourt of the Rotunda. The name, 'the prison of Christ', for this spot would have been given later; I do not know its origin.

IV

THE HOLY SEPULCHRE FROM 1009 UNTIL
THE PRESENT DAY

AFTER the conflagration of the Persians, the fourth-century monument underwent only a few structural modifications. Since the restoration work, carried out in the seventh century by the Patriarch Modestus, there had been a number of partial repairs effected, such as that to the façade of the Rotunda, or the tower erected above Calvary, but, on the whole, there were no important changes. We have to accept that this was so, because of Arculf's evidence. However, the total disappearance of the Basilica of Constantine, in 1009, prevents us knowing what damage was done to it by the fire of 614, or how this was repaired. On 18 October 1009, the Sultan Hakim had commanded the total destruction of the monumental mass of the Holy Sepulchre; and so disappeared the creation of the Emperor Constantine.

The Rotunda and its forecourt, henceforth called 'the Holy Garden', were reconstructed, from 1030 onwards, thanks to the attentions of the Imperial Court of Constantinople, in agreement with the Muslim authorities in Cairo. These works were completed in 1048, in the reign of Constantine Monomachus. The space previously covered by what had been the magnificent Basilica of Constantine was never reoccupied; it remained but an abandoned field of ruins.

1. *The eleventh-century monument*

Some parts of the Rotunda had escaped the pickaxes of the demolitioners, in particular the great circular wall which engirdled it on the west. The reconstruction work of the eleventh century would be organized around this great wall, thereby retaining for the edifice its original form. While a study of the monument as it was in the fourth century has posed a great number of problems, since it had to be rediscovered with the help of ancient remains, the eleventh-century monument will pose many less, for it is partially preserved.

The Rotunda evidently suffered much from the fire of 1808; seven columns out of the ten that existed on the ground-floor disintegrated as a result of the fire, resulting in the collapse of two-thirds of the building. But the repairs carried out by Comnenos did not change the arrangement of the structures, modifying only the internal architectural lines. The drawings of Le Bruyn (Pl. XXIII) and Horn prove that the general aspect was much the same after, as it had been before, the fire; so much so, indeed, that the present restoration work is able, without difficulty, to reproduce the layout of the eleventh century.

Two important novelties were introduced at the time of the rebuilding done by Monomachus; firstly, the large arch of an apse greatly extended the Rotunda to the east, this apse projecting from the façade and encroaching on the courtyard; secondly, an upper floor was added, to which the faithful gained access through a large door opening on to the Street of the Christians to the west. These transformations did not, however, prevent the basic features being restored to the positions they occupied before the demolition. We have seen how, thanks to this continuity, it became possible to reinstate the original layout. But the internal aspect of the Rotunda of the eleventh century, with its two rows of arcades, those on the ground-floor and those above, bore little resemblance to the Roman mausoleum designed by the architects of the fourth century. It is a round church, with a measured rhythm, reminding one of the courtyards of Byzantine palaces.

The great arch is its principal feature. This opens on to the cylindrical shape of the interior masonry; on either side, at the junction of the eastern wall with the circle, the first two columns have not been moved, as is proved by their foundations; only their plinths have been suppressed. Each column has been surmounted with another, two-thirds of its diameter and backing on to the wall. Doubtless, these pieces of column were too short; therefore, twin columns were set upon them, with capitals (Pl. XXIVa) which had been cornerstones of porticos. The sculpturing and moulding of the bases of these features would be of the Ummayad epoch.

To crown the whole, monogrammed capitals of the Justinian period (Pl. XXIVb) formed two great trapezoidal cushions, on which rested the circular stonework of the springings of the great archway. Of all this, only unusable fragments, split and broken, were recovered; they have been copied, and the original pieces placed in the museum. This jigsaw puzzle of reused fragments, taken from the ruins of the City, is typical of the ingenuity displayed by the masons of the eleventh century in reconstructing the Rotunda.

A concha closed the large archway to the east, forming the apse, whose foundations have been rediscovered under the paving of the Katholikon. Its architecture was very similar to that of the church of St. Anne, which must, some years later, have drawn its inspiration from there. When the Crusaders built their church, this apse was removed, and the large archway became the communication-point between the new church and the Rotunda.

All around it, the great deambulatory and the lateral vestibules were vaulted, both on the ground and upper floor; the columns which were put back in place were only fragments of the old ones; their height was diminished by half, hence their clumsy proportions (Pl. XXV). On the voluminous but somewhat rough capitals rested slightly pointed arches. Between one column and another, as well as between the pillars, these formed a row of continuous arcades round the central space; five of them escaped collapse in 1808. Above the cornice, which marks the level of the upper floor, the distribution of the arcades was similar to that on the ground level. However, on the diagonal axes, square pillars took the place of the columns, thereby giving the upper floor a rhythm of alternating square pillars and arches, twinned with a central support column. The nineteenth-century modification of the upper arcades prevented a restoration of this disposition. Above its tambour, perhaps less high than the existing one, the Rotunda was roofed by a timber cone. At ground level, the springings of the vaults were embedded in the great circular wall of the fourth century, preserved together with its three small apses and its windows. On the upper floor, a surelevation, made with salvaged stones, above the frieze of brickwork, carried the upper vaulting. This brickwork fillet, as we have seen, rested on the original masonry.

In spite of the lack of materials, and the enormous difficulties that the reconstruction work of the eleventh century had to overcome, the new Rotunda gave an over-all appearance of great nobility. It bore the marks of a profound religious feeling, with a great mastery of the feeling for proportions. Outside, in the ancient courtyards that had provided light, important buttressing had to be erected to counterbalance the oblique thrust of the vaulting, both that of the ground-floor and that of the storey above; by reason of this fact, the Rotunda was, to some extent, buried.

The Chapel of St. Mary, together with its narthex, is a work of the eleventh century, but the square church of which Arculf speaks must have already been occupying the same site, as a result of the building done by Modestus. To enter the reconstructed church one still passed through the courtyard surrounded by three porticos. Its eleventh-century arcades and columns had been mounted on the old foundations of the fourth century, while, in the south-eastern corner, the reconstructed chapel of Adam backed on Calvary. The beautiful paving which decorated the ground was preserved, but the chapel itself, as well as the one above it, was to disappear during the construction work of the twelfth century, which replaced them, while the original ciborium remained in place. The porticos around the courtyard also had an upper storey, whose walls were preserved, at many points, by the Crusaders. The chapel of Melchisedech, which had escaped destruction by Hakim, was incorporated in this upper storey.

At the south-east corner, up against Calvary and dominating it, an elegant octagonal chapel with a brick cupola silhouetted the far end of the entrance-façade of the monument, for access to the monument was, by that time, obtained by crossing the southern forecourt. This is the existing forecourt, to the west of which a group of three chapels replaced the ancient baptistry; their three small apses, very typical of eleventh-century architecture in Jerusalem, jut out into the forecourt. A row of arcades, resting on columns, marked its southern boundary. On the eastern side, a large, pointed arch, now walled in, opened into an apse, an arrangement difficult to understand. In the cistern under the forecourt, foundation pillars, aligned in a north–south direction, are likewise not easily explained.

Such was the monument that the Crusaders found on their arrival, completed only fifty years earlier. Its magnitude and its quality, the emotion of there worshipping at the Tomb of the Lord, resulted in it not having to undergo any further transformation, except for the apse being removed and, on either side, one of the pillars between the entry doorways was abolished to facilitate passage from the new church to the Rotunda. The existing arches have taken their place.

2. *The church of the Crusaders*

The combination of the Rotunda of the eleventh century with the church that the Crusaders joined to it fifty years later has produced the existing monument. They are clearly two juxta-posed features, but they are not so disparate. Certain indications permit one to think that there existed among the Crusaders a desire for harmonization.

A proof of this is to be found in their use of pointed arches instead of semicircular ones, which were generally used in the west at that time, while pointed arches were, on the contrary, a typically oriental form. Another proof lies in the very pro-nounced eastern character of their sculpture work. It was also fortuitous that the Crusaders brought with them the concep-tion of a storeyed church, which fitted in well with the disposition of the Rotunda.

In the western churches of the twelfth century, the high vaults of the nave and of the transept were buttressed by those of the galleries (Pl. XXVI). These galleries formed an upper floor, overlying the lateral naves of the ground-floor, that is to say, the aisles. The gallery vaulting was, therefore, placed at the level of the oblique point of thrust of the high vaults, thereby serving as a counterforce. Examples of this type of church are numerous; I need mention only St. Sernin of Toulouse, St. Foy of Conques, both in southern France, as well as the churches of Caen in Normandy.

This principle of static equilibrium of construction was applied to the Holy Sepulchre by the Crusaders. The gallery vaults of the upper floor counterbalanced the vaults of the southern and northern arms of the transept, as well as of the triforium above the choir. Originally, they must also have continued around the apse, as is indicated in one of the drawings in the book of Brother Bernardino Amico, who came to Jerusalem in 1593;[1] however, traces of modifications carried out in the second half of the twelfth century on the upper floor to the north of the apse make this questionable.

The type of construction adopted by the Crusaders is, there-fore, of western concept, as is, also, the arrangement of the façade. Western, also, is the type of high vaulting, consisting of vaults on ogival transept-crossings, which were constructed in the first half of the twelfth century, but with a slight difference: the fillets are not under the vaulting, but merge with it. Despite all this, the Crusaders' desire to adapt themselves shows itself in the form of their arches, in the character of the sculpted decora-tion, and in the fact that the upper floor of the church of the

---

[1] Bernardino Amico, *Plans of the Sacred Edifices of the Holy Land*, translated by Frs. Bellorini Hoade, Bagatti, O.F.M. (Franciscan Press, Jerusalem).

Crusaders is on the same level as that of the Rotunda, and that the vaults of the two elements are at the same height.

This adaptation of the Romanesque church to ideas provided by the Rotunda, as it then existed, led to proportions in relation with each other, as well as some degree of unity, which became even more marked, when the arcades on the upper floor of the Rotunda were twinned, in the same way as those that the Crusaders later constructed elsewhere in their church. The cornice which runs around the Rotunda at upper floor level was, likewise, repeated by the Crusaders, at the same height and with the same profile.

I do not think that one can deny a wish to seek unity in all these manifestations. But it is clear that the character of a Romanesque galleried church prevailed, and one cannot but admire the power of the proportions of this medieval transept, which harmonize so perfectly with the grandeur of the earlier Rotunda to which it is joined.

The church of the Crusaders was built in the eleventh-century courtyard, the protruding apse being removed, while the two western support-points of the transept-crossing were sited in close conjunction with the masonry-work of the jambs of the great archway, thereby determining the quadrilateral where the central cupola would be placed. Above the great archway, the stonework of the twelfth century bears traces of a correction, the start of an opening with little columns having been abandoned, and the large medieval ceiling-beam cuts across it. Perhaps the transept-crossing had been conceived in a different manner; in any event, the style of a cupola above a drum on a pendentive, as executed, follows a tradition more oriental than western.

The Crusader building is not only joined on to that of the eleventh century; it also, to some extent, merges with the buildings which surrounded the 'Holy Garden'. The masonry-block of the twelfth-century façade, for example, stops as soon as it surpasses the width of the forecourt; immediately afterwards, the masonry of the eleventh century reappears, joined in the same alignment with that of the twelfth century.

These arrangements occurred as follows: a breach was made in the southern portico of the 'Holy Garden', which, as we have seen, had an upper floor. The medieval façade was then erected in the place of this demolished wall (Pl. XXVII), the interior alignment being that of the eleventh century, as is also the level of the first floor. An extra thickness was simply added to the façade-wall to incorporate the fore-part with its two portals and its two arching windows. The Crusaders even forgot to provide solid foundations for this additional thickness, relying on the ancient foundations, and this was the cause of a slight outward tilting of the façade. The breach being filled by the new façade, the ancient structure continued immediately, finishing at the south-east corner with the octagonal chapel with its brick cupola that I have mentioned earlier.

Here, I would add a word concerning the upper cornice of the façade (Pl. XXII*b*). It is a Roman cornice, of the second century, which has been reutilized—at least, the pieces are not all alike, and one can distinguish two types, very slightly different. Having served as a model for the twelfth-century sculptors, when they were making the cornice which so conspicuously marks the upper floor level half-way up the façade, it was then placed at the top as a crown. The doucine of this Roman cornice was cut, perhaps in the nineteenth century, but, since it was preserved to the right of the fore-part of the building, we have restored it along its whole length, so that the new stone protects the old.

In addition to this feature of Roman sculpture, which, incidentally, is strikingly similar to that of Jerash, the oriental character of the carving on the façade is very clearly evident, with the exception, however, of the frieze which frames the upper bays. Also to the right of the fore-part, the porchway of Calvary, today called the chapel of the Franks, is a detail of high quality; as in the small monument of the Ascension, the corner pillar was covered with marble, the capitals and the columns are also in marble, as well as the sculpted tympanum which decorates the interior of the door leading to Calvary.

On the other hand, inside the church, all the southern arm of the transept is more highly decorated than that of the north, owing to the proximity of the chapel of Calvary, which has since become completely enveloped by the medieval building. Around the northern arm of the transept, the insertion of the Crusader church into the eleventh-century construction is even more noticeable than elsewhere; the northern portico of the 'Holy Garden', together with its arcades and its vaults, is preserved, completely integrated with the twelfth-century architecture surrounding it (Pl. XXVIII*a*).

In the gallery of the upper floor, the eleventh-century northern wall was slightly modified by the insertion of four windows, reinforced with columns (Pl. XXVIII*b*). Since this wall had to carry the springing of the vaults, this insertion was an imprudence on the part of the medieval builders. The old wall was too weak, and, moreover, its masonry was of bad quality; under the thrust of the vaults, the wall fell outwards. The resulting disorder was among the most serious of the repairs which had to be made in the church.

One notices, on the left-hand side of the forepart of the façade, that a window was obstructed as long ago as the twelfth century by the construction of the tower, the moulding and the capitals of whose windows were already out of character with the rest. Likewise, in the interior, during a second campaign of building operations, a monumental gateway was inserted into the deambulatory, the style of which, typical of the twelfth century, is so beautiful. This opened communication between the church and the Canons' cloister which, in the second half of the twelfth century, came to occupy the abandoned space where the Basilica of Constantine had stood. Today, this cloister has become the courtyard of the Abyssinian monastic quarters, which are so thrilling, and is dominated by the strange silhouette of Comnenos' apse.

The cupola of St. Helena's crypt came out in the Canons' cloister which was, as it were, built around it. The crypt had been arranged in the first half of the twelfth century, before the cloister, and Ummayad capitals were reused in it. There were five others in the church; that of the northern transcept-arm and those of the transept-crossing. These several pieces are of great quality; the masons of the twelfth century, like their predecessors of the eleventh, also knew how to reuse beautiful pieces which they found in the ruins. In addition to these Ummayad capitals, there were also ancient columns, sixth-century capitals, and others, even older, which probably came from the ruins of Constantine's Basilica. All these diverse elements, tastefully reassembled, give a very attractive character to the Holy Sepulchre. An attempt at modern sculpture has not, unfortunately, integrated at all well, while the ancient and Romanesque sculpture make such harmonious neighbours.

The Holy Sepulchre is, for those who love it, like a book in which many pages of the history of Jerusalem are written. Certain passages are transcribed *en clair*, in plain language; for example, everything said by the Rotunda is easy to read; other pages are almost obliterated, but one can still divine their meaning. One can see, for example, the size of Constantine's nave in that of St. Helena's crypt, as also the plan of the Basilica in that of the cloister, since its southern wall is the wall of the Canons' refectory, while its northern wall is that of the dormitory. Because ancient foundations have been reused right up to our own time, all this is still outlined in the area.

But what the Holy Sepulchre can still most movingly tell us, is of the fervour of all Christian peoples for the Tomb of their Saviour. This fervour shines before our eyes, and becomes evident when one discovers, overlapping one into the other, all these monuments which have been raised by men to the glory of the Resurrected One.

Every age has left its testimony writtten in stone: it is this history book whose pages I have ventured to leaf through with you.

Jerusalem
3 November 1972

INDEX

PLATE I

(Photograph: American Colony, Jerusalem)

Façade of the Holy Sepulchre before 1914

PLATE II

PLATE III

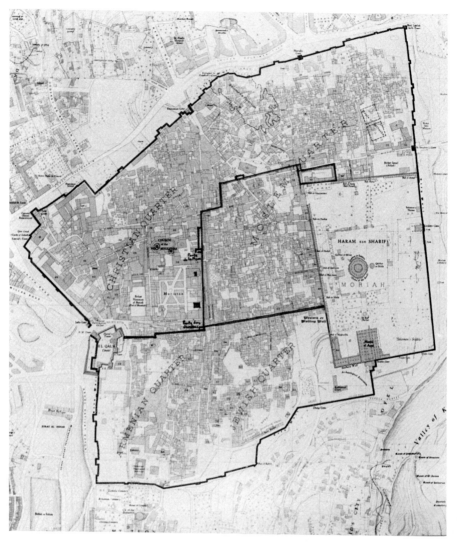

The line of the wall (the 'second Wall') marking the northern limit of the City at the time of Herod the Great

PLATE IV

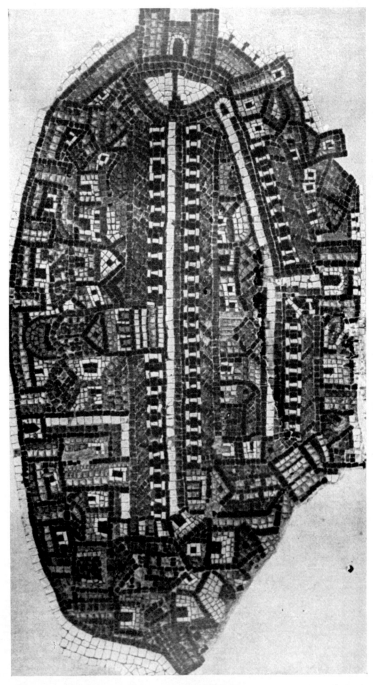

The plan of Jerusalem according to the mosaic Madaba Map (*after P. M. Gisler, O.S.B.*)

PLATE V

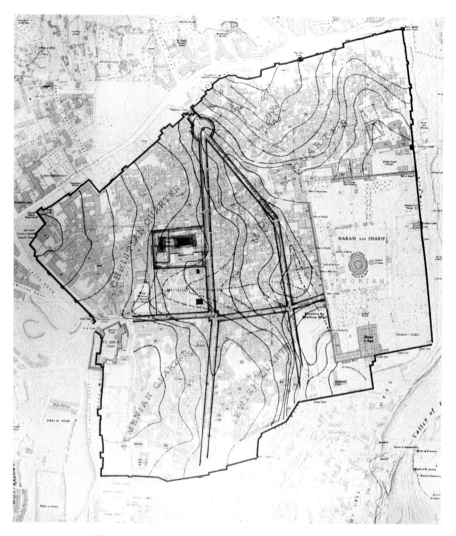

The Cardo Maximus and the Forum of Aelia Capitolina

PLATE VI

(Photograph: Denise Fourmont)

Representation of the fourth-century Edicule on one of the Monza Flasks

PLATE VII

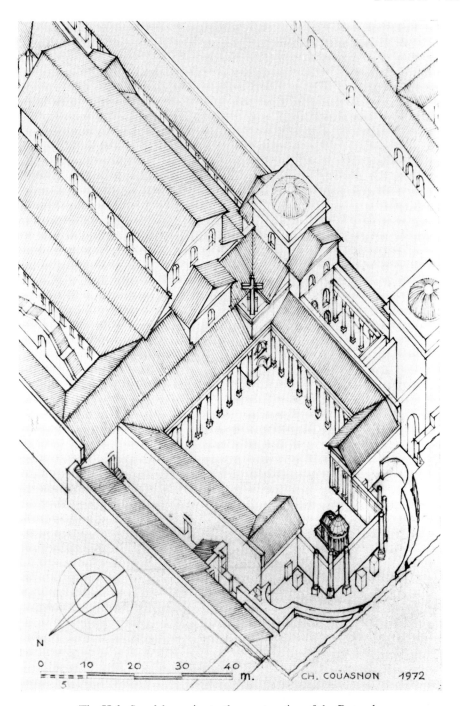

N

0   10   20   30   40
    5   m.   CH. COÜASNON   1972

The Holy Sepulchre prior to the construction of the Rotunda

PLATE VIII

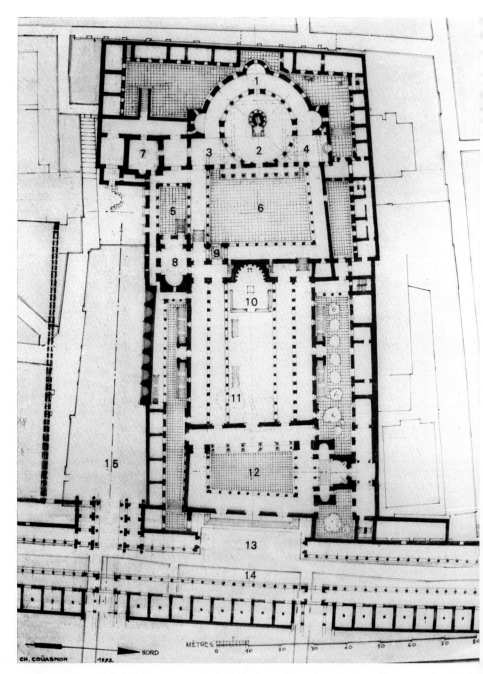

Reconstruction of the complete plan of the Holy Sepulchre at the end of the fourth century: (1) Ambulatory; (2) Rotunda; (3) and (4) lateral vestibules; (5) southern atrium; (6) courtyard of the Rotunda; (7) Baptistry; (8) Church of Golgotha; (9) the Cross; (10) Basilica of Constantine; (11) the crypt of St. Helena; (12) eastern atrium; (13) entrance; (14) Cardo Maximus; (15) site of Hadrian's Forum

PLATE IX

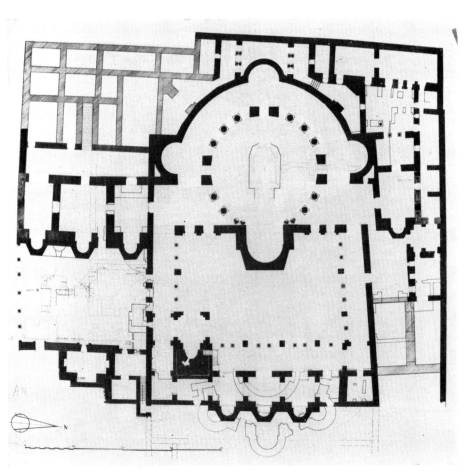

Plan of the edifice rebuilt in 1048

PLATE X

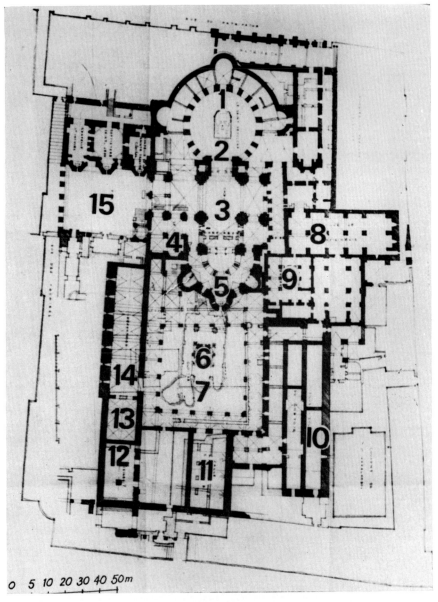

Plan of the Holy Sepulchre in the twelfth century: (1) Edicule of the Tomb; (2) Rotunda; (3) Katholikon (transept and apse of the twelfth century); (4) Calvary; (5) apse; (6) crypt of St. Helena; (7) cloisters; (8) to (14) Monastery of the Canons; (15) entrance pavement

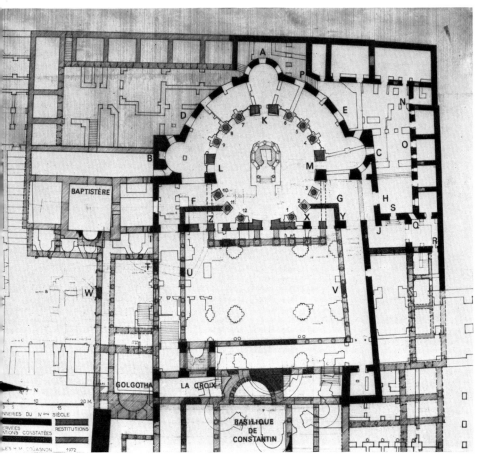

PLATE XI

Plan of the Rotunda and its surroundings indicating stone work and foundations of the fourth century

PLATE XII

a. Foundation-stone of column no. 2

(*Photographs: B.T.C.*)

b. Foundation-stone of column no. 3

PLATE XIII

Photographs: Valentine Trouvelot

b. Vaulted passage (P on Pl. XI) between the northern and western courtyards

a. Cell door (O on Pl. XI)

PLATE XIV

(*Photograph: Valentine Trouvelot*)

Arch of the northern vestibule (G)

PLATE XV

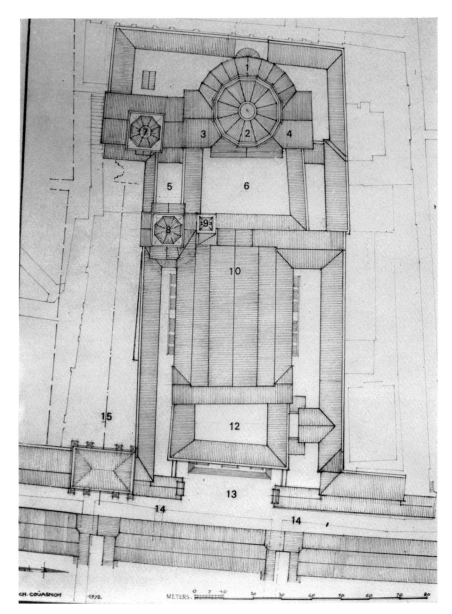

Roof plan of the fourth-century Holy Sepulchre: (1) Ambulatory; (2) Rotunda; (3) and
(4) lateral vestibules; (5) southern atrium; (6) courtyard of the Rotunda; (7) Baptistry;
(8) Church of Golgotha; (9) the Cross; (10) Basilica of Constantine; (12) eastern atrium;
(13) entrance; (14) Cardo Maximus; (15) site of Hadrian's Forum

PLATE XVI

b. Northern vestibule, pillar M

(*Photographs: B.T.C.*)

a. Foundation-stone of column no. 12

PLATE XVII

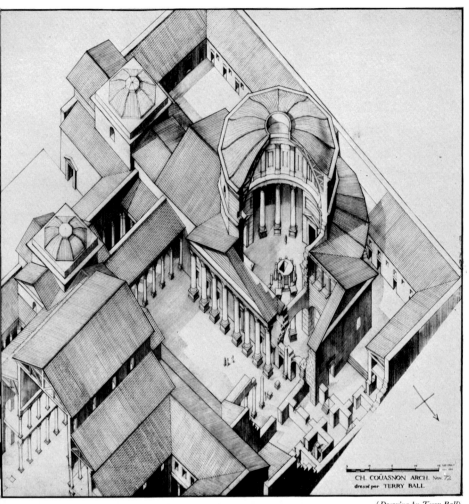

CH. COÜASNON ARCH. Nov 72
dressé par TERRY BALL

(*Drawing by Terry Ball*)

Reconstruction of the fourth-century Rotunda

PLATE XVIII

(*Photograph: Valentine Trouvelot*)

Columns nos. 2 and 3 freed of their supporting masonry

PLATE XIX

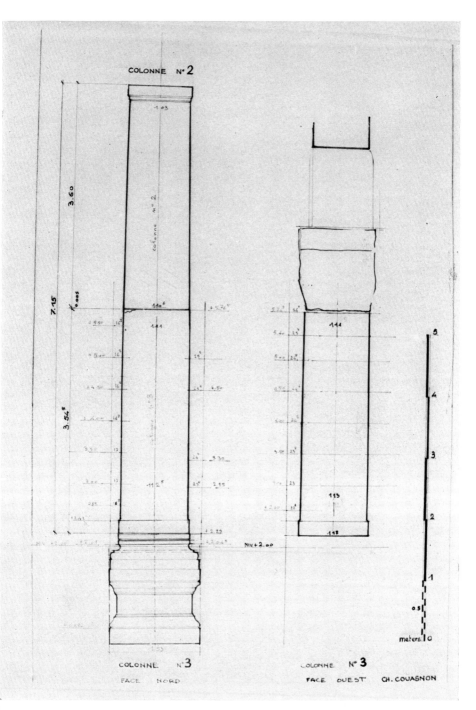

Reconstruction of a fourth-century column in the Rotunda

PLATE XX

b. Foundations of the apse of the Constantinian Basilica with remnants of the pavement of the eleventh-century gallery (to the left)

a. Traces of reworking near a doorway of the fourth century (X on Pl. XI)

PLATE XXI

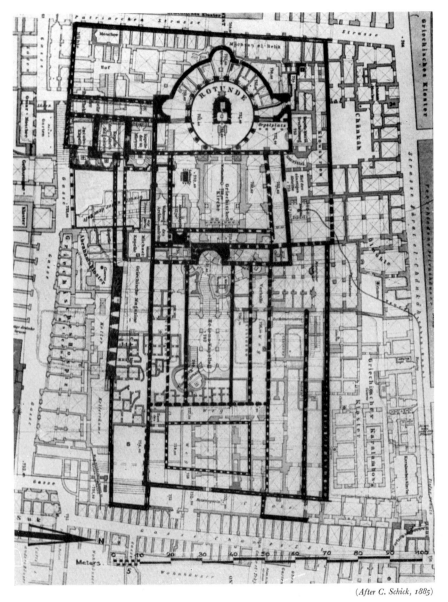

(After C. Schick, 1885)

Traces of the foundations of the Constantinian Basilica in the Holy Sepulchre quarter

PLATE XXII

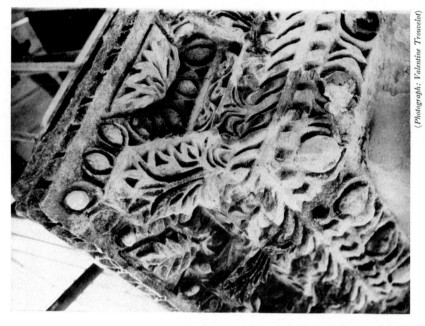

(Photograph: Valentine Trouvelot)

b. The angle of the Roman cornice surmounting the twelfth-century façade

(Photograph: Palestine Museum)

a. The northern jamb of the central doorway of the entrance atrium of the Constantinian Basilica

PLATE XXIII

The eleventh-century Rotunda according to the drawing of Le Bruyn, *Voyage au Levant*, 1725

PLATE XXIV

a. Umayyad leaf-capitals reused in the eleventh-century edifice

(Photographs: B.T.C.)

b. Monogram on a sixth-century capital reused in the eleventh century as filling above the previous capital

PLATE XXV

(*Drawing by Terry Ball*)

Reconstruction of the edifice rebuilt in 1048 by Constantine Monomachus

PLATE XXVI

(*Photograph: Valentine Trouvelot*)

The southern arm of the transept of the twelfth-century church

PLATE XXVII

(Photograph: B.T.C.)

The recently repaired twelfth-century façade of the Holy Sepulchre (1972)

PLATE XXVIII

(Photograph: Valentine Trouvelot)

b. Upper gallery in the northern transept

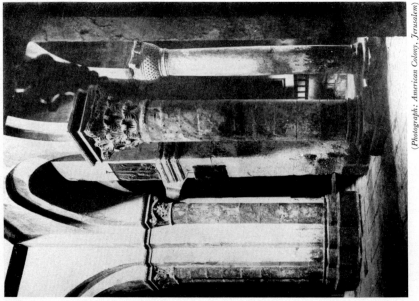

(Photograph: American Colony, Jerusalem)

a. Juxtaposed columns of the eleventh and twelfth centuries in the northern arm of the transept